Parenting Difficult Children

Parenting Difficult Children

Strategies for Parents of Preschoolers to Preteens

Michael Hammond

ROWMAN & LITTLEFIELD
Lanham • Boulder • New York • London

Published by Rowman & Littlefield
A wholly owned subsidiary of The Rowman & Littlefield Publishing Group, Inc.
4501 Forbes Boulevard, Suite 200, Lanham, Maryland 20706
www.rowman.com

16 Carlisle Street, London W1D 3BT, United Kingdom

British Library Cataloguing in Publication Information Available

Library of Congress Cataloging-in-Publication Data

Hammond, Michael (Psychologist)
Parenting difficult children : strategies for parents of preschoolers to preteens / Michael Hammond.
pages cm
Includes index.
ISBN 978-1-4422-3847-3 (cloth : alk. paper) -- ISBN 978-1-4422-3848-0 (electronic)
1. Parenting. 2. Parent and child. I. Title.
HQ755.8.H33353 2015
306.874--dc23
2014021734

♾™ The paper used in this publication meets the minimum requirements of American
National Standard for Information Sciences Permanence of Paper for Printed Library
Materials, ANSI/NISO Z39.48-1992.

Printed in the United States of America

For Trish—with all my love
(to the moon and back!)

Contents

I

Building a Secure Foundation

It is said that there are two primary tragedies in life. The first is not receiving everything that you think you want; the other is to receive everything you think you want. Those of us who are parents may feel, at times, much the same way. We desperately love our children and could not imagine our lives without them; and yet, there are moments when we feel angry, frustrated, or alienated from our child and may even wonder why we had children in the first place. Fortunately, for most of us, these negative feelings are fleeting and evaporate quickly from our minds. And then the kid deliberately tests our patience when they do some obnoxious or defiant behavior that makes us want to scream, and we are back into the negative thought loop.

In my clinical experience, it is not that the vast majority of parents of young children do not *wish* to parent their children consistently and well, it is that they often do not know *how* to parent their children consistently and well. This is especially true for parents of young (ages 3–12) children who have difficult temperaments and are frequently in opposition to their parents' requests and demands.

These kids want their own way. They expect to receive what they demand. They are routinely inconsiderate and obnoxious. They will use whatever weapon they have in their behavioral arsenal to try and bend the parent to their will. If pleading, crying, and begging do not provide immediate relief to the demand, they will escalate to arguing, name-calling, threatening, and—not infrequently—aggression to get their way. And, as often as not, they *do* get their way because the harried parent wants the child's behavior to stop. Just stop. You've had all you can stand.

When the difficult child gets their way the oppositional/defiant behavior does stop—and the parent does feel some badly needed relief; until the child once again hears the hated "no" word and the coercive, destructive, relationship-destroying cycle—the parent/child anger dance—starts over again. This is no way to live. This is no way to parent.

ADAM

I once was asked to see a married couple in their late twenties for family therapy. The focus of their concern was the tension in the family and the anxiety symptoms that the mother was attempting to cope with. When I first spoke to the mother and then the father on the phone, I requested that they tell me a bit about themselves and the composition of their family. They sounded quite ordinary. The father was an accountant, the mother a former music teacher. They lived a comfortable middle-class lifestyle. They had one child, by choice, a son named Adam. I requested that the parents come to the first appointment without Adam so that I could focus more precisely on the couple and their troubles. The father responded that they would be glad to come to the first appointment without Adam—if they could still find a sitter. I suspected that Adam was at least partly involved in the tension in the family. I was right, but I didn't know at the time how right I was.

After taking a mental health and personal history, I asked the parents to tell me about their lives. They had friends but rarely socialized with them. Although they lived nearby they saw their extended families once or twice a year. They were religious but rarely, if ever, attended services. They had no hobbies or personal interests that they enjoyed. Their groceries and dry cleaning were delivered. They could not remember the last time they took a vacation, went out to dinner, went to a movie, or engaged in any recreational activity other than watching television at home.

And the reason for this peculiar behavior? Adam. "Tell me about Adam."

They looked at each other, they looked at the floor, they looked at their shoes, the mother began to weep, and then the father looked at me sheepishly and responded, "We don't do anything that Adam doesn't decide for us." Adam decided what the family was to have for dinner; what TV shows to watch; what time to go to bed; whom and when they could see others; what, if any, recreational or personal activities the parents could enjoy, and so on.

The parents freely admitted it. Adam controlled their lives. Adam did not do anything that Adam did not want to do. Adam was five years old.

How did Adam become the ringleader of this particular circus? In a word, fear. The parents were afraid of Adam. I asked the pertinent question. What did two twenty-something functional adults have to fear from a five-year-old child?

The mother explained this time. "You have no idea what Adam is like. If Adam doesn't immediately get his way about *anything and everything* he flies into a rage. He screams, he cries, he threatens, he throws, he hits. He tears the house apart. And there is no compromise with Adam. Everything must be exactly as he wants it to be. Then, and only then, will he stop raging."

The father piped in, "Adam's rages are like a volcano. It is a meltdown times ten. It is easier to just give in and let it go. We have no life other than the one that Adam permits. Yes, doctor, we freely admit it, Adam is the master of our lives."

Adam was a pint-size tyrant and an anarchist. He had his parents buffaloed and right where he wanted them. He was a five-year-old master of his domain and wasn't about to give up his throne. Why was Adam this way?

As I told his parents, Adam's world was out-of-control because his parents refused to exert control of Adam. He may appear to be entirely happy with his exalted station in life, but just the opposite was true.

He had the enormous weight on his shoulders of being the sole authority in charge. He made all of the family decisions because the parents were afraid to exert their authority for mortal fear that Adam would rebel. With no trustworthy, limit-setting adult in charge, Adam felt like he was living on a runaway train heading for calamity—which of course, he was. The resulting anxiety for Adam was mind-boggling. What a terrible burden for a little boy to bear.

The parents protested. "Doc, you don't understand. The one and only way to have any peace in our lives is to let Adam have his way. You cannot discipline Adam. You cannot reason with him. You cannot ignore him or divert his attention. If you give him something like candy or a toy to get him to stop, he grabs it and then goes right on with the fit. The pediatrician says that there is nothing medically wrong with him. We can't enroll him in school. I can't stand the meltdowns and I can't stand to see him so unhappy. He is just a little boy and he is going through a stage. Don't you think he'll outgrow it?"

No, I responded. I did not see that Adam was going through a stage and that he would eventually outgrow it. Adam was the way he was because his parents permitted it. The parents did not willfully and knowingly set out to raise a tyrant; they just took no definitive steps to prevent it.

I explained that when Adam was an infant he was completely helpless and dependent on his parents and caregivers to provide every need. When Adam was hungry or uncomfortable or needed changing, the parents responded. The parents rocked him, changed him, bathed him, played with him, fed him, and showered affection on him. As well they should have; we would expect nothing less. When done well, the infant's impression is that the world is a safe and consistent place that can be depended upon. This parental behavior continues at a steady pace until the child is around age two.

And then adults begin making demands on the child. This is when the little royal actor first discovers that they are not the center of the universe. People do exist apart from solely satisfying the child's every need and want. The parent has a life, and wants and needs, too.

Sometimes they have to wait. Sometimes they have to be patient. And worse, the parent sometimes refuses the desired behavior and says, "No." "No, leave that alone, don't touch!" "No, take that out of your mouth." "No, cookies are all gone until after dinner." "No, you must wait your turn and share." "No, you must pick up your toys and put them away."

Surely, you are not referring to me? Oh, the horror! The miscarriage of justice! The need to loudly protest! And when they do refuse and protest, the parent has the power to terminate the unwanted behavior by not allowing it to continue.

We all learn the hard lesson that there are limits to our behavior, that other people have wants and wishes too, that we must follow rules and expectations, that all behavior has consequences, and that we will not receive everything we want when we think we want it. That is unless the child is not taught these things at the age of two, and the child is indulged and pampered and spoiled. When this happens they learn to fear that the world is indulgent to the point that no one really cares enough to stop me from doing only that which I wish to do. A world without limits produces anxiety that the world is not dependable and safe. Anything goes.

The difficult child's defense is, No, the world *does* revolve around me and my every wish is my command. And if you try and breach my castle I will use every arsenal at my disposal to dispel you of such a foolish notion. If you try to limit me, I will limit you first. If you try to dissuade me, I will dissuade you from even trying, and if you punish me, I will punish you for doing so. Adam.

I told the parents that they had a choice. They could choose to continue to indulge Adam, perpetuate his delusion that every choice in his life was his alone, and continue to live in chaos and misery, or they could reassert their authority and become Adam's parents and not his captive drones.

The parents protested it was not that they *wanted* Adam to run the show; it was that they did not know *how* to reassert themselves as the child's parents. The answer was to learn exact skills to consistently and effectively parent a difficult child. This is what Adam's parents did, and today he is a happy, successful teenager without emotional meltdowns.

There is no magic involved. There is no need for painstaking years of complex family therapy to unearth unconscious insights into the why of your child's behavior; no need for special schooling, harsh punishments, complex interventions, or medication breakthroughs. What is needed then and now is to learn common sense but commonly used behavioral parenting skills that have been researched and proven time and again to be consistently effective in altering the defiant and oppositional behavior of young children. That is the purpose of this book.

These same behavioral parenting skills are equally effective in *preventing* the occurrence and establishment of demanding and obnoxious behaviors of young children. If you do not want to raise a brat but a responsible, trustworthy child who has a loving relationship with his or her parents, these skills will be of tremendous help. Regardless if your child is heaven sent or hell bent (or is more likely most of the time somewhere in the middle) this book can help you be the parent that you want to be and have the child that you want to have.

This book is full of tools and skills for every level of difficulty with young children (ages 3 to 12), from minor irritations to major disconnection between parent and child. Please keep in mind that not *every* skill is for *every* parent. You'll need to choose according to your own situation. You can do this in several ways:

- Read the book cover to cover, using all of the skills that apply to your situation.
- Read the parts that you like and apply those skills; disregard what you do not like.
- Use the book like a toolbox; take it out when you need an answer to a problem.

Part I covers behavioral tools that help families function well. You will learn how to construct rules and consequences that are consistently effective. Part I also covers communication, encouragement, and active problem solving. By using these skills collectively, you will be able to guide and direct your child through their younger years with great success.

Part II presents time-tested solutions to a variety of problems, some simple and minor (but no less irritating and disruptive to family functioning) and some serious enough to threaten your child's well-being and the parent-child relationship. Choose what you think is relevant to you and what you find useful.

The most important thing is to know that you *can* change how things are going in your home and with your child. *Believe* that you can, put your trust in the skills that you are about to learn, and apply them with ever-increasing confidence. Do this and you will see the results that you want. I have taught thousands of parents to use these skills and tools effectively. They can be just as effective for you.

One thing to note: When I have given talks about using these parenting skills to parents of young children I am always asked, "Well, what about when the child becomes a teenager? Then do you need a different set of parenting skills?" Yes, you do. Parenting a teenager is different than parenting a younger child. Fortunately, the behavioral principles are the same. Many of the skills are also the same, but their application is sometimes different than it is for young children; and some of the skills and issues only apply to kids at that age. If you have teenage children, or you want to learn the skills to parent them when they do become teenagers, I have written another book called *Decisive Parenting: Strategies That Work with Teenagers*, also published by Rowman & Littlefield. Some of the same content and concepts have been repeated in this book. Either book can be of tremendous help. Now, let's go to work!

Note: Please note that there are several worksheets referred to within the text that can be downloaded from the computer website for this book, decisiveparenting.com. These items are as follows:

- Discipline Plan Worksheet
- Rules Tracking Guide
- Problem Behavior Checklist
- Problem-Solving Worksheet
- Daily Class Assignment Report
- School Behavior Checklist
- Community Behavior Checklist

Chapter One

Rules 101

Establishing a Firm Foundation

Rules are basic to family life. Rules form the firm foundation for a discipline plan. Establish firm and fair rules and discipline will follow naturally from them. This is especially true for parents of young children. Children need to experience firm and fair rules from their parents as soon as they are old enough to understand them.

If children are not expected to follow rules and expectations from a young age, imagine what they very likely will be like when they become teenagers. Further imagine these children as adults. We all know adolescents and adults who are self-involved, obnoxious, and irresponsible. To a large extent the breeding ground for their behavior has occurred when they were children and their parents had few, if indeed any, good rules for their behavior that were consistently enforced.

Rules are best when they are based upon your family values—the standards you believe are important to follow. Such values provide a moral compass that helps the child find his way. When you think about it, most parents want their children to be—regardless of age—responsible, trustworthy people who make decisions in their behavior that reflect their family's values. That is why as parents we need to be careful about the rules we have for our children.

When rules for children are unnecessary, unclear, unfair, or unenforceable, anger and chaos quickly develop. The *absence of clear expectations* causes friction between you because your child doesn't know what you expect of him or her. So rules need to be constructed deliberately and carefully. Before we begin to construct rules, here is what a rule is and is not.

DEFINITION OF A RULE

A rule is different from a hope, demand, or expectation. Here is an example of a *hope*: "I wish that you would do all of your homework before going out." This says that you would *prefer* that he do the homework.

A *demand* is more like a rule but has an unwanted personal aspect: "You will do all of your homework before going out." However, a demand, such as this, is personal and sets up a power struggle with your child.

An *expectation* is not demanding enough "I expect that you'll do all of your homework before going out" provides no consequence other than failure to meet the expectation.

"Before you go out, complete all of your homework every night that it is assigned" is a *rule*. It tells the child what to do and when to do it.

So the first thing to know about establishing rules is that you want to avoid stating a hope, a desire, a personal demand, or expectation. A rule states exactly what and when you expect your child to do something. Rules are the home's version of society's laws that regulate public behavior. None of us can do as we please when we like. Good rules, like good laws, prevent chaos.

"RULES" FOR DEVELOPING RULES

There are five rules, or principles, for the development of a rule.

1. Focus on behavior, not attitudes.
2. Write down the rule; say it aloud often.
3. Tie the rule to a set consequence.
4. Involve your kids in devising rules.
5. Monitor compliance with the rule consistently.

Rule 1: Focus on Behavior, Not Attitudes

Behavior can be seen or detected. You can see that your child has cleaned her room, fed the dog, or did not come home past a set time. You can see by the evidence of her behavior if she has complied with the rule about cleaning her bedroom, feeding the dog, or coming home on time. You cannot have a clear understanding of her *attitude* about complying with the rule. She may not *like* the necessary behavior or your demand to stop the prohibited behavior, but that is not the issue. The issue is whether or not she is in compliance with the rule—regardless of how she feels about it. When she is in compliance, be sure to praise her and encourage the behavior to be repeated—which goes a long ways towards helping most people change their attitudes.

Having a rule such as "improve your attitude toward your sister" is pointless. What is it that you want your child to do or not do? How will he or she know she has done it? If you want him to stop hitting his sister, you need to say that. A rule such as "never hit your sister" focuses on the behavior that you can see or detect and not on an attitude that you cannot see.

Rule 2: Write Down the Rule

Rules are much more likely to be observed when we write them down. You can post them in final form in a prominent place, such as on the refrigerator or the bathroom door. Give your child a copy of the rules, retaining your own copy. This procedure prevents arguments later over exactly what the rule states. If there is dispute about who does dishes on Mondays and Wednesdays—or is it Mondays and Thursdays?—you have the written form to refresh everyone's memory.

It's a good idea to repeat the rule as necessary. You can say the rule is: "Wash all the dinner dishes every night that you're assigned." Your kids will likely pick up on this quickly and say, "Yeah, I know, the rule is wash all @#$%^ dinner dishes every night that you're assigned. You don't have to tell me." That's just fine because your child has internalized the rule—even if he or she doesn't like it.

You can write the rules down and repeat them to your child until you're blue in the face, but if there is no follow-up on the rule, it is a colossal waste of time and energy. To help you follow up, you'll need to tie the rule to a set consequence.

Rule 3: Tie the Rule to a Set Consequence

When children know beforehand that if they choose to break or disregard a rule an unpleasant consequence will follow, they are much more likely to follow the rule. But too often kids choose to gamble. They gamble that they can get by with breaking the rule, or that you likely will not enforce it. Sometimes they gamble and lose. You find out about the wrongdoing and decide to discipline your child. But often your child can get by with a warning, or get through the confrontation with pleas, yelling, threats, and promises. This brand of inconsistency breeds contempt for rules and for discipline when it does come.

A more effective alternative is to clearly identify what your child will lose if she chooses to gamble on rule enforcement in the first place. Don't let her guess. Don't hope that you can think of some really good consequence after the fact. Instead, clearly identify the consequence that is built into the rule.

With this method, your child has certain knowledge that if she chooses to break the rule, she is choosing the consequence that is part and parcel of the rule. This helps her develop consequential thinking, a critical skill, for now she knows if you choose to do A, B will follow as surely as night follows day. I call these rules "consequence rules," and they are the only type of rule you'll need. Here are two examples:

Rule: Put all dirty clothes into the hamper.
Consequence: Clothes that are not in the hamper will not be washed.

Rule: Finish your homework every night that it is assigned.
Consequence: Stay home that evening to finish uncompleted homework.

We will explore in depth what kind of consequences to use and how to enforce them in later chapters.

Rule 4: Involve Your Child in Devising Rules

It is a good idea to involve your child in devising new rules and changing old ones as necessary. People take much better care of things they have had a hand in constructing than things they haven't.

Sit down with your child and explain your concerns about a particular behavior and the need for a rule to change the behavior. Ask for her input and opinion. Some kids cannot or will not participate in this process. If your child refuses to have input, tell her that's fine; you'll go ahead without her. Then go ahead. Most kids will quickly realize it is to their advantage to be involved, because they are more likely to have the rule turn out to their liking. The advantage to you as the parent is that you'll likely get considerably less resistance to the rule when your child is directly involved in its construction.

Rule 5: Monitor Compliance with the Rule Consistently

Consistency is the key to success in establishing and gaining compliance with rules. A rule will quickly float away like a breeze on a hot night if the parent enforces the rule one day and disregards it the next. Children learn very quickly from experience that the rule is of little value and can be safely ignored. They will think, "Mom and Dad don't really care about enforcing the rule, so why should I be concerned about following it?"

Consider the family where the child is told to be home by a set curfew. She is compliant for a day or two. On the third day she decides to test the rule and comes home half an hour late. Her parent gives her a dirty look and tells her to always be home by curfew. The child is home by curfew the next three nights, and stays out two hours late on the fourth night. Her parent yells and threatens. She stays out two hours late the next night. This time her parent looks at her in disgust and doesn't say anything about the curfew rule. Thereafter, the child stays out as late as she likes. And the rule? With no consequence or rule enforcement, the rule has drifted away on the night air.

HOW MANY RULES DO YOU NEED?

Some families have a difficult time because they have too many rules. When you have too many, the importance and the need for any one rule is lost in a sea of regulation. Kids don't need a rule for every behavior under the sun. Parents who try to micromanage every aspect of their kid's behavior day and night invite rebellion.

It is very hard for both parents and children to keep track of multiple rules. However, it can be disastrous to have too few rules, or worse yet, no rules. The solution is to have a few rules, ones that are necessary, fair, clear, enforceable, and consistently applied.

SUNSET RULES

Rules should have a beginning and an end. You wouldn't think of having the same rule for crossing the street for your fifteen-year-old as you would for your five-year-old. When a rule is no longer needed, it should die a natural death. Either circumstances or your experience with the child make the rule unnecessary. I call these rules "sunset rules" in that they have a "sunset clause" when the need for the rule has passed. However, some rules will be in effect in one form or another for years—rules about attending school or completing chores for example. When do these rules formally sunset? When your son or daughter is no longer living at home or no longer dependent on you, the rule sunsets.

Now we are ready for the task of deciding what rules your family needs and learning how to construct them so they will provide a secure foundation for the parent-child relationship. If your rules are weak or nonexistent, hang on. Help is here!

Chapter Two

Rules 102

More Ways to Establish a Firm Foundation

Now that we know what a rule is, let's talk about the important components of a good rule. There are four essential *characteristics* of a rule. A rule needs to be necessary, fair, clear, and enforceable. To make it enforceable, we combine it with a known consequence. First, however, let's talk about how to make sure the rule is necessary, fair, and clear.

Necessary Rules

A rule is necessary when there is a difficult or problematic or unacceptable behavior that needs to change. A child who hits their sibling in the head once in a blue moon does not have the same level of problem behavior as a child who does this constantly. A child that never brings their homework assignments from school does not have the same issues as the child who does not bring schoolwork home on occasion. The child who ignores set chores, or does a poor job completing them, does not have the same level of problem behavior as the child who skips out on a chore once in a while. In the latter instance you can handle the problem without a rule. In the first instance you certainly do need a reasonable rule about never hitting anyone, or always bringing homework home, and completing chores.

The yardstick to measure the need is the *frequency* and the *intensity* of the problem behavior. How often does the behavior occur? How big a problem is the behavior when it does occur? Behaviors that occur frequently and are intense are good candidates for modification through rules.

Fair Rules

A rule needs to be fair to be effective. When it comes to rules they don't like, kids frequently say, "That's not fair!" which can be translated, "That's not the way I want it to be." By fairness I mean it is something that the child is capable of doing to comply with the rule. A four-year-old cannot be expected to clean her room to a high standard; a twelve-year-old certainly can. A fair rule is also within the bounds of common sense. It is neither fair nor reasonable or likely to happen when we have a rule that a child will do three hours of homework every night, especially when the child has never done a minute of homework a day in their life.

A rule is especially fair when one person's behavior directly affects the rights of others and is for the common good. Fairness often depends upon your perspective. A child may say, "I should be able to play with my toys anytime and anyway I want to—they're my toys." However, from an adult perspective a rule about use of toys is fair because toys are to be respected and used appropriately. Toys are not to be used in combat. Toys are not to be stepped on. Toys are not to be left out in the rain. Toys are only for play that hurts no one and that can be used again for the natural life of the toy. Now, it is also fair that if you really don't care how your child chooses to use their toys, or you don't mind replacing lost, stolen, or broken toys at will, or conversely, your child appreciates and takes good care of their toys, then do not make use of toys a rule.

There are different rules and expectations for different people at different ages and under different circumstances. Your five-year-old will not get to do or have certain things that a ten-year-old will; likewise the fifteen-year-old. With more freedom comes more choices, and also more responsibility to make appropriate choices. Your five-year-old may have a fair rule such as, "At the crosswalk, always hold Mommy or Daddy's hand, as we wait for the green light to cross." By the time the child is ten the rule may be, "Always wait for the green light to cross." At fifteen, the rule about crossing the street is no longer necessary, and it is no longer fair to have it (at least we hope not because this is something the child is capable of doing, and has long since internalized the rule).

Of course adults have rules too. We can't drive down the road any way we like. We must pay obligations. We must treat each other in a civil and lawful manner. And the more often our children see us obeying rules and expectations, the more likely it is that they accept the fact that they too must follow rules that are necessary and fair.

Clear Rules

A rule must be clear to be effective. The best way to be clear is to use words that describe behavior that the child can understand. The rule, "Always let me know where you are and when you'll be back" seems clear until you think about it carefully. You may have a clear idea of what you mean, but your child may or may not. The rule is subject to interpretation as follows:

- *Always.* Always is fine. Always means always.
- *Let me know where you are.* Let you know how? A written note? Phone call? Email? Text message? Smoke signal? Do we want the child to tell us just where they are—at the neighbors? Across town? At Jimmy's house (who is Jimmy and is there responsible, adult supervision?).
- *And when you'll be back.* At sunset? 9:00 pm? When they feel like returning home?

With this unclear rule the child can leave a vague message about their whereabouts, nothing about the circumstances of where they are, choose what time they will be back, and still comply perfectly with the unclear rule of, "Always let me know where you are and when you'll be back." Children are frequently Philadelphia lawyers and are looking for loopholes that allow them to interpret a rule to their advantage. The easiest way to avoid misinterpretation is to write the rule simply and clearly. "Always ask permission in person or by phone if you wish to leave the house, where you'll be, and what time you will be back."

Enforceable Rules

A rule on notification of whereabouts is fine, but it is pointless if it is not enforced or is unenforceable. Devising a rule will not necessarily alter your child's behavior any more than a posted sign will deter speeders. After one or two speeding tickets, however, most of us will hold the speed down, at least on the section of road where we got the ticket. So it is with kids. Children will need consistent sanctions for breaking the rule. But when sanctions are given sporadically, or not at all, the child learns that he can get by with breaking the rule. He then strives to find out each time if this is a time he can get by with breaking the rule. This doesn't mean that the child is "bad"; it is just human nature to see what the limits are in a given situation. A rule based on behavior you can see can be enforced with consequences. A consequence is the thing that happens next after you choose a behavior, and all behavior has consequences.

WATCH YOUR LANGUAGE WHEN WRITING RULES

A rule can be necessary, fair, clear, and enforceable and still crack and creak like a foundation infested with termites. There are some important guidelines to follow when enforcing rules that will help prevent failure before you even begin.

One of the strongest weaknesses in the rule occurs when it is constructed using accusatory or demeaning language. Directives like "Because you're such a pig, always clean up your room" and "Since we can't trust you, come home from school immediately" are disrespectful and do nothing to build a positive relationship between you and your child.

Using authoritarian language in the rule will likely invite a power struggle. Rules that begin with the word *you* are authoritarian: "You will," "You shall," and "You must." Listen: "You shall be home by 6:00 every night"; "You will do all of your homework every night it's assigned"; "You must take out the trash can to the curb every Monday night." Kids, just like everyone else, are usually more cooperative when they believe they are being treated with respect, instead of being ordered around like drones.

Now listen to the revised rules: "Be home by 6:00 every night"; "Do all of your homework every night that it is assigned"; "Take out the trash can to the curb every Monday night." The rules have lost none of their clarity or authority. Your child may still not want to do the task, but she is less likely to feel personally offended by the rule. The word "you" makes the rule personal. Depending on how I feel about you and you about me, I'm likely to take that into consideration when I hear "you" in the rule. "Oh yeah? We'll just see if I do it or not. They can't tell me what to do!"

Note that none of these rules are a request or a desire. They are requirements. Requirements are not offensive in and of themselves. If we want something to happen, we must meet the requirements. When the child enters school they quickly learn that recess for them will not happen if they do not make an effort or misbehave in class. Class time effort and positive behavior is a requirement for recess. If they want to play sports, they must meet the team requirements to participate. If they want to spend the night at a friend's sleepover, they must meet the hosting parent's requirements as well. We must all meet the requirements to do or have certain things throughout our lives. And there is nothing wrong with parents requiring certain behaviors from their child.

There is also nothing wrong with stating requests or desires to your child. A request or desire gives your child the option of doing it or not doing it; there is a choice. For example, "Would you clean out the hamster cage before you go to the movies?" is a request; the child may or may not clean the cage before leaving. "Clean the hamster cage every Saturday morning before you take your shower" is a rule. The rule, in contrast, offers no choice.

Notice that in the examples above, each rule has one behavior. A rule such as "Take out the trash can to the curb every Monday night, and then come back in and sweep out the garage, and then empty the cat box, and then go back into the house and do all of your homework before watching TV" is confusing and burdensome. If you want the behaviors behind each of these rules altered because they are a consistent problem, you'll need a separate rule for each behavior. To summarize, there are four guidelines for the language you should use when writing a rule:

1. Leave out accusatory or demeaning language
2. Do not begin a rule with *you* as that invites a power struggle
3. Do not write a request or a desire
4. Focus on one behavior per rule

WRITING RULES

A good way to start a rule is to use either an action word, such as "go," "clean," "begin," or a time element, such as "When you come home from school . . ." or "As soon as you are out of bed in the morning . . ." or "By 6:30 each evening . . ." Another good way is to use the words "always" and "never," as in "always do . . ." or "never do . . ."

Practice writing out the rules you want and saying them out loud. Ask others if they think the rule sounds right, and if they think the proposed rule will do what you want it to do. Watch for loopholes or how the rule can be misinterpreted.

Here are a few representative rules that parents have constructed in my parenting classes. See if you can pick out the ones that meet all of the rule criteria (especially the ones that are necessary, fair, clear, and enforceable) and which ones need an overhaul.

- Act your age.
- Go to school.
- Do what you're told.
- Attend all of your scheduled music lessons after school.
- Don't talk so long on the phone.
- Stop arguing.
- Always ask permission before using my tools.
- Do three hours of homework every night.
- Limit your calls to ten minutes and three calls an evening.
- Don't play video games all night.
- Never argue, discuss.
- Stop hanging around those people.

- Spend money wisely.
- Play video games for no longer than one hour on school nights.
- Stop hitting your brother.
- Never hit your brother (or anyone else).

These are the "good" rules from the list that meet all of the criteria:

- Attend all of your scheduled music lessons after school.
- Always ask permission before using my tools.
- Limit your calls to ten minutes and three calls an evening.
- Play video games for no longer than one hour on school nights.
- Never hit your brother (or anyone else).

Because of the way that they are constructed, the others are unclear ("Act your age"), unnecessary, ("Spend money wisely"), unfair ("Do what you're told"), or unreasonable ("Do three hours of homework every night"). Some of the rules have all four problems.

WRITE YOUR OWN RULES FOR YOUR CHILD

1. Identify Problems

Make a list of the problems you are having with your child. (For help, see box 2.1, the Problem Behavior Checklist; this checklist is also available on the website). Use action words (behavior that you can see). Write down as many problems as occur to you. Do not try to analyze or come to a conclusion about *why* your child acts that way, just write down the problem.

2. Prioritize Problems

Review your whole list, considering the *frequency and intensity* of each problem behavior. How often does the problem behavior occur (frequency) and how big a problem is it when the behavior does occur (intensity)?

3. Edit the List

Draw a line through those behaviors that have occurred infrequently or are not so important at this time. Now look at your list. You should have two or three problem behaviors you especially want to work on. If you have four, five, or more go over the list again and prioritize the top three. These are the ones you want or need to see behavior change on right now.

　　If you are parenting with someone else, compare your lists. Choose the top three problem behaviors the two of you can agree to work on together with your child. If you cannot agree on an item, ask a third party whose opinion you both respect to help you decide. If you still cannot agree about one or more items, ask the other parent to back you up as you work with your child on changing that problem behavior. If your partner refuses to help you in any way, you can go it alone, or you can consider eliminating the behavior from your list.

4. Check the Criteria of Necessary, Fair, Clear, and Enforceable

Now consider, if you were to construct a rule with a set consequence for noncompliance (the "consequence rule") for each behavior problem you identified, could you make the rule meet these criteria: is it necessary, fair, clear, and enforceable? If not, you may need to rethink the rule in behavioral terms.

5. Engage Your Child

Sit down with the child (if you can) and explain your concerns about his or her behavior using your list of two or three areas. No matter how immature you think your child may be, if they are old enough to understand what a behavior "rule" is ask for their input and opinion.

6. Finalize Your Rules

Write a consequence rule using the "Discipline Plan Worksheet" provided on the website. Look the rule over to make sure it deals with one behavior and is clear, fair, necessary/reasonable, and enforceable.

7. Brainstorm Consequences

Tie the rule to a specific consequence or a series of consequences. Accomplish this step collaboratively with your child, if possible.

8. Go Live with the Rules

Put the rule into effect; let your child know that from now on there is a rule and a consequence for not following it. Write down the consequence rule and post it where the child will see it regularly.

9. Monitor Compliance

Track compliance with the consequence rule using the "Rules Tracking Guide" provided on the website.

10. Review and Revise

Revise or add new consequence rules as you need them, always to remember to have only a few rules at a time.

PARTNERSHIP BETWEEN PARENTS

Even though your child may be cooperative about following rules you construct, what should you do if one parent favors a rule but the other does not? What should happen if Dad wants a consequence rule for washing dishes after snacks, but Mom doesn't really care? What if Mom wants a consequence rule for playing video games, but Dad doesn't care if the kid has an "all-nighter" once in a while? Here are some guidelines for you to follow: Be sure the rule is not only wanted, but also necessary. If it is necessary, is it also clear, fair, and enforceable, and written in behavioral terms that everyone can understand? Are you willing to take a stand for the rule, and to follow through consistently in enforcing the rule?

If you can arrive at a "yes" for all three questions, go forward. Here is what you can do.

> The best way for families to work together on establishing rules is to come to an *agreement*. You talk and listen to one another with caring concern and agree to take a stand on the rule. You then seek the input, cooperation, and agreement of your child. Most kids will want to have input on the rule. Welcome their input because they are more likely to cooperate if they have had a hand in constructing it. This is true of young children (over the age of five) as well as older ones. When a child refuses to have anything to do with rule construction, you say, "Fine, we'll go ahead without you. And the rule still stands." Then go ahead.
>
> If both parents cannot agree on the rule, then the parent who wants the rule must agree to be the primary agent for enforcing the rule. The other parent who doesn't care that strongly about the rule must agree to back up the parent who does feel strongly. The rule may not be what one of you would like, but you're willing to concede to your partner's wishes and support the rule.
>
> Both parents and the child may talk over the rule and find areas that can be negotiated and compromised on, while still retaining the essence of the rule. This is coming to an *accommodation* about the rule. A useful alternative is for the parents to contact a third party whose opinion is respected by *both parents* and ask for his or her suggestions. This could be a friend, a relative, clergy, a therapist, or an advice columnist.

The rule may need to be rewritten at this point. This means coming to a *consensus* about the rule.

Finally, you can *ditch* the rule; do away with it. If both parents cannot work together in any of the ways listed, it is better to give up on the rule and permit the child to do as he or she sees fit in this or that behavioral area. This is bad policy for your child, and it teaches nothing about compliance, discipline, cooperation, and respect. However, it is better than continual family feuding and conflict. Having no rule is also preferable to having a rule that one parent may undermine because he or she doesn't really believe in it. If Mom wants a firm bedtime on school nights and Dad says, "As long as their grades are up, what does it matter?" will there likely even be a rule to enforce? If parents routinely disagree on what rules to have, it may mean the family has some serious problems. At this point, seek out a family therapist to help sort out the situation.

The best way for families to work together on establishing consequence rules is to come to an agreement. The next best way is to come to an accommodation about the rule. The third way is to come to a consensus. Finally, ditch the rule if there is no other way. In most families where love and caring exist, there is a way. The reason for family rules is because we love our children. Love makes the way.

PROBLEM BEHAVIOR CHECKLIST

Make a list of all of the behaviors that your child is currently doing that are a significant problem. Consider the *frequency and intensity* of the problem behavior before you add it to your list. Does the problem behavior occur with increasing frequency, and is the problem behavior intense when it does occur? Add any problem behaviors that are not on the list, but relevant to your situation. Complete a separate list for each child whose behavior concerns you.

Around the House:

leaving dirty clothes/dishes lying around
getting up too late/staying up too late
arguing with parents
emotional meltdowns
arguing
backtalk
fighting with siblings
"borrowing" family members' belongings

misuse of the phone
not completing chores
misuse of television, stereo, computer, or electronic games
unacceptable level of hygiene
poor manners

School-Related:

not completing classwork or homework
playing video games instead of doing homework
failing grades
being late for school
wearing inappropriate clothes
disrespectful to school staff
cheating
bullying

Out and About:

notification of whereabouts
coming home after a set time
staying out overnight without permission
involvement with negative friends
misuse of skateboard or bicycle
lying
choice of friends/associates
violent or fighting behavior
shoplifting, stealing
vandalizing property

other _____

REASONABLE GUIDELINES AS ALTERNATIVES TO RULES

One last important point about rules. There are a few behaviors where the perspective rule would meet all of the criteria for a consequence rule, but the enforcement of it would be pointless. These are matters of the heart: rules about attending religious services, engaging in charitable work, or the child having contact with an absent parent with whom he or she has emotional issues. You will not win your child's allegiance by having a rule for these behaviors—especially for older children. You may say what you would *like* to have happen, based upon your values, but this is fundamentally different from the demand through a rule.

Does that mean you should never require your kid to do something he or she might find unpleasant? Of course not. It depends upon the circumstances, the age of the child, and your family values. If you cannot abide your child *not* engaging in certain behaviors that you require, there is nothing wrong with that. But you should exercise discretion at times. Likewise, in some cases you can encourage and support your child to make the decisions that you would prefer, but will respect her choice, as difficult as that may be for you.

It is also a waste of time to set rules for things that will likely be thrown over for something new. Hairstyles, clothing, music, and other things that involve personal taste and preference will change as your child gets older. You could set rules for hairstyle, clothes, and music, but what would be the point? Instead, you can set *reasonable guidelines* for your child to follow. He or she may choose within those parameters. Yes, some kids will want to comb their hair into spikes. Some kids will want to combine gaudy makeup, ragged clothes, costume jewelry, and combat boots. And some kids will want to listen to music that will drive their parents up the wall—and then the next week they are back to their former hair style, wearing conventional clothes, and listening to 1950's rock. By the time you are ready to do battle, the war is over. Choosing your battles with care is a very good idea. Reasonable guidelines help you avoid unnecessary scrimmages that will only exhaust you. For example:

- Craig can play video games, but only ones with prior parental approval.
- Susan can wear a T-shirt to church as long as there are no references to drugs, bands, violence, profanity, or Satan.
- Aaron can listen to any band he likes, but not to gangsta rap or hardcore metal.

These behaviors may still not be what you would like, what you would prefer, but as long as they do no harm, they are harmless. Even if the child dresses like a rodeo clown after a rainstorm, and listens to music with blasting guitar riffs, and screaming incomprehensible lyrics, it is better to let it go on these than to give in on critical issues that do involve your child's welfare, safety, or well-being.

Well, what if the child's choice does involve his or her welfare, safety, or well-being? For example, should you permit your child to consume a heavy diet of sugar? Or have contact with strangers? Or listen to profanity-laced, sexist, and/or racist music? Your child could become seriously ill, or be sexually assaulted, or have his or her mind polluted. For most parents, this kind of restriction on their child's behavior comes under the heading of reasonable guidelines. You may need to set limits and veto choices over the limits, but if you do, be prepared to monitor and supervise compliance. It may not be easy. Saying no and meaning it rarely is.

In chapters 3 and 4, I will show you how to choose an effective consequence, tie it to the rule, and to enforce it. Rules rule!

Chapter Three

Natural and Logical Consequences

As discussed in the last chapter, attaching rules to appropriate consequences is one of the key elements of successful rule-making. There are three kinds of consequences we use in this book: natural, logical, and active. This chapter discusses natural and logical consequences; active consequences will be covered in chapter 4.

NATURAL CONSEQUENCES

A natural consequence is one that happens naturally as a result of the child's action without the parent having to do anything. It comes about as part of the natural order of things. For example:

- If I spend all of my allowance at the video arcade, I don't have the money to go with my friends to the movies.
- When I don't ask my parent to sign my Boy Scout permission slip in time to go on the camping trip, I stay home.
- If I don't get my clothes in the hamper on washday, I wear my cleanest pair of dirty underwear.

Natural consequences are predictive of the kind of sanctions the child will face as an adult for making illogical or irresponsible choices—as long as you don't step in and rescue him from the effects of the natural consequence. Natural consequences provide good opportunities to learn that when you choose a certain behavior, you're choosing the consequence that goes with it. Natural consequences are very effective learning tools for that reason.

The parents don't have to do anything to make natural consequences happen. But they do have to refrain from "rescuing" the child from the consequence. It can be a temptation to, for example, get on the phone with the scout leader and plead for the child to go on that field trip. But if the parent does that, the child misses the opportunity to learn to think ahead and choose more carefully. There will be exceptions, of course, but parents should avoid rescuing a child too often.

LOGICAL CONSEQUENCES

A logical consequence is one that is arranged beforehand by someone and is logically related to the misbehavior. The consequence is devised by the parent for the child's experience as a result of his behavior choice. The logical consequence works best when it is tied to a consequence rule, although it can be devised on the spot if necessary when your child engages in an unexpected misbehavior. Here are some examples of logical consequences:

- If I use your tools without permission, the tools are locked up until you are satisfied I can use them, clean them, and put them away properly.
- If I leave my bike in the driveway, I am grounded from using my bike for two days.
- If I get a ticket for not wearing my bike helmet, I lose the use of the bike for a week. If I get a second ticket, I lose the use of the bike for a week and then can only ride it under direct parental supervision for another week.
- If I go to a prohibited site on the Internet, I have no computer use for a specified period and then I can use it only under supervision.
- If I let a friend talk me into skipping math class, I get extra homework tonight and two extra pages of math problems on the weekend.

Here are some types of logical consequences that parents can put in place.

Confiscation and Forfeiture

Confiscation and forfeiture are two types of logical consequences. They mean that when a child chooses to make an inappropriate choice, he or she pays a price. This involves confiscation or forfeiture of items or services:

- If you leave your skateboard out in the driveway, I'll confiscate it for three days the first time, seven days the second time, and ten days the third.
- If I find your toys scattered and abandoned on the living room floor again, I'll confiscate them for three to ten days, depending.
- If I find pornography or weapons or drugs, I'll confiscate them permanently.

Confiscation works very well for kids who are forgetful or lazy or have things that they should not have. Forfeiture can be used to deter insolent or defiant behavior. Take away a possession as a cost. Tell your child you will not play a game of "catch" (back and forth). The first time you need to take away a possession because of insulting or uncooperative behavior, it will be donated to charity.

Make the item small and something that is not personal (not a memento of a trip or a gift from a friend or beloved relative). Make a "hit list" of such possessions so your child will know what to expect if she keeps it up. Give away the CD you have bought, a movie pass that was to be given for cooperative behavior, or the weekly allowance. A kid at the homeless shelter will be tickled to get any of these items. You can also take away routine favors or services you do for your kids, such as driving them to the mall or permitting use of your resources, your time, or your money.

You want to get your child's attention and cooperation and show that you mean business. Confiscation and forfeiture are very effective means of transacting such business.

Overcorrection

Another behavioral technique that can be used as a logical consequence is overcorrection. Your child must "practice" a behavior until he or she has it right. If a skateboard is left in the driveway, have her put away her skateboard three or four times in a row. When he runs in and slams the door, have him go out and come back in several times without running and slamming the door. When he yells and has a cursing fit, have him repeat himself until he can speak to you or someone else in a polite and calm manner. Repeat the task until it is done satisfactorily. Most kids hate overcorrection, and many learn to do better the first time.

Response Cost

Response cost is a common behavioral technique that is used as a logical consequence. The idea is simple. If the child chooses the "wrong" behavior, they lose a privilege; if they choose the "right" behavior they gain a privilege. You can make a list of such "wrong" and "right" behavior choices and give a copy to your child. If you choose the "wrong" behavior of ignoring your afternoon chore list, you choose to stay in the house with no recreational activities until they are done. If you choose to torment and tease your sister (or anyone else) you choose to give your weekly allowance to the sister, or to charity. The reverse is also true: if you choose the "right" behavior you gain the privilege, or even more.

Community Service

You can't think of an appropriate logical consequence for a certain misbehavior? Then have your child perform a number of hours of community
service. Have her volunteer for a shift at the church food bank. Have him
tutor younger children at the community center. Have her pull weeds from
the elderly neighbor's garden. Community service works well because, while
the loss of time and freedom is unwanted and serves as a deterrent, the child
is likely to feel good about his or her contribution.

CONSEQUENCES FOR OCCASIONAL MISBEHAVIOR

Consequences are a key part of rule-making. But, of course, not every infraction is related to a rule. Can you use a logical consequence in connection with
a misbehavior for which you have no consequence rule in place? Yes, this is
best for when misbehavior is not an ongoing problem, rather one that happens once in a blue moon.

- If I break the window, I need to pay restitution and help install a new
  window.
- If I swear at the teacher, I need to make a formal apology.
- If I come home three hours late for the second time, I'll be given a small
  amount of freedom out of the house until I gradually earn back all of my
  free time.

The key point in using a logical consequence as a discipline tool is the
consequence will be most effective when it is tied to a consequence rule, that
is, it is set beforehand and is logically related to the misbehavior. Occasionally, misbehavior will happen for the first time or will be so infrequent that you
don't need a consequence rule. On these occasions, I advise you to arrange a
logical consequence on the spot, as long as it can be logically related to the
misbehavior.

Review the list of problem behaviors you wrote down while reading
chapter 2. Practice devising a logical consequence for each of the behaviors
you listed.

NATURAL AND LOGICAL CONSEQUENCES AT WORK

Lee

Lee was hungry. He had missed dinner the night before and now he was
ready for a big, hearty breakfast. He had just finished combing his hair just
the right way so it would look cool practically the whole day. By the time

Lee got to the breakfast table, his mother was picking up the last of the breakfast dishes and putting them in the sink. Lee was puzzled.

"Where's mine?" he asked. "Didn't you wait for me?"

"Good morning,," his mother said.

"Where's breakfast?" Lee asked again.

"Breakfast is at 6:30," his father announced. "It is now 7:10. Everybody is leaving in five minutes.."

"But I didn't get any dinner!" Lee protested. "I was at Ben's house last night, and just now I was doing my hair."

"Uh huh," Lee's mother said. "Dinner is at 6:00. You came in at 7:00."

"You wouldn't even let me make a lousy sandwich last night."

"And we said that we would see you for breakfast at 6:30," Lee's mother said.

"Do you hate me? Think I'm fat? Is this some kind of Korean thing?"

"You'll have to wait till lunch," Lee's father said.

"It's not fair!"

"It's time to go," the father said.

"Would you like a piece of leftover toast and a glass of milk to take with you to the bus stop?" Lee's mother asked.

"No, that would look stupid," Lee replied.

Lee walked heavily out to the bus stop. He could hear his stomach growl as he thought about what mean and unreasonable parents he was stuck with. That evening Lee washed his hands and helped set the table. He smiled broadly when dinner began at 6:00.

Vicky

Vicky had worked hard on mowing the lawn and trimming the bushes. This chore was above and beyond her regular routine of chores, and she was doing it to earn some extra money from her parents. They had agreed to pay the minimum wage. Now she was anxious to collect her $12 and go shopping. She was surprised when her mother handed her a $10 bill.

"Uh, Mom. It's actually $12. That's how long I worked."

"I know it's $12, dear. I subtracted $2 for the maid service."

"Excuse me?"

"For the maid service; today is wash day."

"We don't have a maid, Mom."

"That's right. You remember that I told everyone in the family that I was going to charge $1 for every article of clothing I found lying on the bedroom floor on washday?"

"Okay, Mom. I get the point. Can I have my $2 now?"

"Not this time, Vicky. If you want maid service you have to pay for it. It's only logical, don't you think?"

The next washday Vicky scoured her bedroom for any clothes that had been left on the floor—or anywhere else—and dropped them into the hamper. She thought it quite amusing when her brother was charged $3 for two dirty socks and a pair of underwear.

Steve

Steve was a little worried about the traffic ticket. He'd only had his new bicycle a month, and this was already his second ticket. The cops were out to get kids on bikes, that's all. Everybody else was riding on the wrong side of the street. Steve knew that his dad would go ballistic and yell, but after that was over he'd tell them to be "more careful" and then would pay the fine for him. It wouldn't be too bad.

"Dad? I got another stupid traffic ticket. Can you take care of it?"

"What was the ticket for?"

"Oh, riding my bike on the wrong side of the street. You know how cops lie in wait for you."

"Were you riding on the wrong side of the street?"

Steve hesitated before answering. He was a little puzzled. This was usually when his dad started swearing and yelling. Steve's dad looked at him with a calm expression. He had completed a "Decisive Parenting" course at the high school just three days before.

"Well, yeah, sort of," Steve answered finally.

"Do you remember that we established a consequence rule about riding your bike?"

"Yeah."

"What is the rule?"

"I don't know, something about following traffic laws."

"The rule is obey all of the traffic laws."

"Okay, so?"

"And what is the consequence that goes with the rule?"

"Dad, come on . . ."

"That you'll pay all of your own traffic fines and that you'll lose the free use of the bike for two weeks for every traffic fine you receive."

"Come on, Dad. You can't be serious about that stuff."

"You'll need to pay your own fine. And you'll either not ride, or your mother or I will monitor when you use the bike for two weeks. Paying your own fine is a natural consequence of getting a ticket, and losing the right to ride is only logical. Which of the two options would you prefer?"

"I don't have any money! You've always paid for stuff before."

"That's okay; we can find some jobs for you to do. Do you want to have us monitor your bike riding by riding along, or lose the bike for two weeks?"

"Ride along. At least I can still ride. But do I really have to work?"

"Son, welcome to the real world."

Steve shoveled snow from all of his neighbor's walks. He cleaned out the garage and refinished his mother's oak dresser. In two weeks' time he had enough money to pay his traffic fine. For two weeks his parents monitored whenever Steve wanted to use the bike by riding along with him. After the two weeks were over Steve did not ride on the wrong side of the street even when his friends urged him to do so. He didn't get another ticket for nine years.

Chapter Four

Active Consequences for Challenging Situations

At some time all kids defy their parents. Remember when your child was two and their favorite words were "no" and "mine"? Much the same mentality will apply from time to time now that your child is older. Periods of rebelliousness are normal and to be expected.

DEFIANT-BEHAVING CHILDREN

Most kids resist consequences some of the time, but what about the child who doesn't respond consistently to discipline through consequences most of the time? This is not a *bad* kid; this is a *defiant-behaving* kid. Defiant-behaving children defy rules and adult authority almost without fail. If this is your child, you need a unique set of parenting skills to change his or her behavior. This chapter and the next will teach you these skills.

Defiant, irresponsible behaviors look like these:

- Eli says "So?" or "I don't care" when you lay out the consequence for his misbehavior. Take away his Play Station for a week? "Go ahead—keep it; I didn't want the stupid thing anyway."
- Julia resists discipline by pretending that rules and consequences don't apply to her. She is special. She is above that sort of thing. When consequences for misbehavior do come, she is incredulous that you are so blind and brainless, that you don't understand rules only apply to lesser mortals and certainly not to her. "I am twelve. I can do what I want, see?"
- Paul engages in unacceptable behavior habitually: he wants to use your wallet as an ATM machine; sees nothing wrong with turning his bedroom

into a toxic waste dump, and thinks that skate boarding over ice-covered
streets is an acquired skill. To top it off, a kid like Paul will try to mini-
mize his involvement in wrongdoing. After all, he put the fire *out*, he
returned the bike after a *week*, and he only knocked the little kid down
once.

- Elizabeth abhors taking responsibility for her behavior. It's the other kid's
  fault. It was circumstances beyond her control. She wanted to do the right
  thing, but people and circumstances forced her to do the wrong thing.

Children who engage in these kinds of behaviors typically lack two
things: insight into reasons for their behavior and empathy for those whom it
affects. When asked, "Why did you do this?" a common answer is "I don't
know; I just did." As they frequently act on impulse and emotion, they often
cannot give you a logical explanation why they engaged in some particular
misbehavior. "I don't know. I just did" is therefore a truthful response. Setting up a logical consequence beforehand for the child to experience fails to
change behavior because these kids often don't think ahead.

The same is likely to be true with their ability to learn from the natural
consequence. These children are not considering the consequences and the
ramifications of their behavior for the next day or next week. They are
concerned with doing what they want to do, when they want to do it, and the
hell with you or anybody else that gets in their way. After it happens is when
they first think about the resulting injury, expulsion, or criminal charges—
and even at rare times with older children—the consequences of sexual or
drug experimentation.

In addition, because their wants and needs come first, these children often
hurt other people. Just as these kids lack insight into why they do what they
do, it is hard for them to consider what might be the effects of their actions
on others. They're not thinking about the possible trouble and misery for
their parents and other people. Some kids have such weak attachments with
their parents and others that they also *don't care* about the effects of their
behavior.

THE ACTIVE CONSEQUENCE

Since the more common natural and logical consequences often do not work
very well or for very long with these children, what can you do instead?
What works consistently well with the child whose behavior is so defiant or
irresponsible is the active consequence. This type of consequence restricts
the child's *freedom*. The active consequence is a freedom-restricting consequence brought on by your *child's choice*—she chooses to have you involved
by virtue of the poor choices she makes. You take over making good choices

for your child until she proves able to do so. *You take a very active role, sometimes long-term, in fulfilling the consequence you or others apply to your child's behavior.*

Parents should consider using active consequences when they *know* their child has a consistent history of defiant behavior. For example, if you feel your child's friends are less than desirable and you restrict your child from seeing them without just cause, contact with these friends will automatically become more desirable in your child's mind. His friend is now forbidden fruit and becomes an object of considerable want and need. If, on the other hand, you have evidence of repeated shoplifting or some other irresponsible behavior when with this friend, you have just cause to closely monitor and supervise the contacts with her friend, or restrict access to the friend. Until when? Until your child demonstrates by her behavior she has become trustworthy.

Active parental involvement is the essence of the active consequence, as compared to no involvement whatsoever in natural consequences, and no involvement beyond devising the consequence in logical consequences. Any child whose behavior is habitually defiant or irresponsible can be moved to a position of assuming personal responsibility for his or her behavior with time, commitment, and the diligent application of a sound discipline and behavior change plan on your part. Using active consequences you can and you will have good success.

HOW TO SET THE ACTIVE CONSEQUENCE INTO MOTION

The active consequence consists of physical action and mental attentiveness on the parent's part. You will use any or all of these actions (active consequences) to ensure compliance on your child's part:

1. Intercession
2. Networking
3. Tracking
4. Monitoring
5. Supervision

Your intention in using these five skills is to form an open hand, not a clenched fist. Like natural and logical consequences, the active consequence is designed to help, not to hammer, to provide the opportunity to teach and to learn. It is your tool of choice when the other two kinds of consequences don't do the job.

INTERCESSION

Intercession involves being an active mentor to your child, or finding help related to altering his or her behavior problem. Sometimes the child needs information—such as why a particular behavior is unacceptable or prohibited. Sometimes, our most effective action is to step back and ask others to step forward. There may be times when you need someone else to dig at the roots of your child's behavior problem, rather than trying to trim back the branches.

The child may be consistently misbehaving in some part because he has a psychological or medical condition and won't be able to change his behavior until that problem is addressed. The child may need to see a psychotherapist to talk through his problems and learn some new skills. He may have a medical condition that requires medication help to alter his behavior. He may need to see a physician, an optometrist, or an audiologist in order to feel better or to see and hear better.

Early Warnings Signs of Problem Behavior

There are early behavioral signs that your child may be heading for trouble. Any one of these signs alone may not be enough to indicate a problem. When you see several together and in a consistent pattern, you should follow up. Talk to your child and tell him or her what you have seen. If this is not successful, you may want to talk to a competent family therapist or mental health therapist who can help you and your child sort things out. The professional can make recommendations about what should happen next. The behavior to look for includes the following:

- Loss of interest in school: (for middle school children) skipping classes; incomplete assignments, failing grades
- Loss of interest in usual activities: hobbies, clubs, sports, time with family
- Loss of interest in friends: not returning phone calls, not going out with friends, friends not contacting the child
- New friends your child doesn't want you to meet
- Becoming secretive or lying to parents about whereabouts and activities; having large sums of money or unexplained gifts
- Refusing to discuss with parents or other adults what is happening in their lives
- For older children, increased interest in things that are overtly antisocial, such as some kinds of violent movies, music, and games; worrisome clothing or hairstyles, jewelry, body art, language, and gestures; putting up offensive wall posters and reading offensive materials

·

- Significant changes in mood and/or physical appearance, sleeping or eating habits, and ability to concentrate on everyday activities; being "sick" more often than usual; unusual weight loss
- None of these signs *alone* necessarily indicate a serious or consistent problem. Your child may be merely trying on a new image, and some of the things may be a matter of personal taste and preference that can be handled under the heading of *reasonable* guidelines.

A consistent pattern of several of these behaviors occurring together over a period of time, however, may indicate a serious problem is about to arrive—or is already here.

Special Intercession

Some children have biologically based mental health disorders that require specialized assessment and treatment. Disorders such as Attention-Deficit Hyperactivity Disorder (ADHD) or Attention Deficit Disorder (ADD), as well as Bipolar Disorder and Autism Spectrum Disorder, are not uncommon with children who have difficulty controlling their behavior. The same may be true with children who have explosive tempers. Some kids have experienced significant personal trauma that has impacted their behavior in ways in which they "act out" their distress. Some children develop clinical depression or anxiety disorders. A few kids are addicted to drugs and alcohol—yes, even at a young age this can happen—and need immediate assessment and treatment. This may mean outpatient or specialized long-term care in a hospital or treatment facility. A number of rebellious or troubled kids become actively suicidal or self-abusive. Such self-abuse requires immediate specialized assessment and intercession on your child's behalf.

You can also be an active intercessor for your child in other areas. You can actively cultivate a relationship with your "difficult" child by practicing the communication and problem-solving skills presented in later chapters of this book and by showing your love in active ways. You can also note that, in fact, your child could be acting out family stress and dysfunction. In this case, your family may need the beneficial intercession of family therapy. Further, some kids are enmeshed with delinquent friends or associates and need specialized intervention to leave the lifestyle behind. Sometimes your child needs academic help. Many kids become rebellious about attending school and doing homework because their academic self-esteem has been beaten down by a sense of failure and rejection. Many kids with irresponsible behavior have learning disabilities that have not been identified and dealt with through their school years. Interceding by providing tutoring help and remedial work can be a tremendous benefit for such kids. Further, many schools now have adult mentor volunteers to assist kids who need help. Accessing available help is active intercession for your child.

NETWORKING

Networking means gathering and sharing information with the places and people your child is involved with on a daily or frequent basis, such as the school, day or after school care sites, clubs, religious centers, or agencies. It may also include sharing information with family members, other kids who know your child, and especially with his or her friends' parents. You want adults in your network who know your child, who work with your child, or who love your child.

Does networking mean you're going to share intimate details about your child's life with anyone who asks? Certainly not. Does it mean you are going to be gathering and disseminating certain information about the child? On a need to know basis, yes. For example, are you going to tell her friends that she was molested? No. Would you tell her therapist that? Yes. It is information that could help account for her behavior. Would you tell her teachers about the rules you have for her completing and turning in her homework? Yes. It is information that is relevant for the teachers to know. If you know and trust your child's principal, teachers and school counselor, coaches, youth pastor, juvenile probation officer or caseworker (if she has one), and your child's friends' parents, you can share and gather information that will be consistently useful to you in helping your child. The same may be true for adults in your neighborhood, who may know your child less well, but have information about the child's behavior that you want to know. You may also want family members in your network—grandparents, aunts, uncles, cousins, and others, who can share what they know in regard to your child's behavior.

- If my child is consistently not turning in school assignments, I want to know that.
- If my daughter, who is becoming a habitual thief, comes to the community center wearing a new leather jacket she "found behind the gym," I want to hear about it.
- If my youngest son, who likes to hit people, is seen assaulting another child in the hallway, please call me at once.

Is that asking people to spy and snitch on my child? No. It is asking people to report what they see, letting me make the decision about whether the information is important or not. Further, you're providing information about what you know so there is mutual sharing. If you think your child is involved in a negative peer group, or is a "wannabe" member, ask the network to look for signs and activity. Any child who is skipping classes, bullying others, cheating in class, or engaged in criminal activity will have a much harder time doing so when his or her parents have the support of a personal network helping you look over the kid's shoulder.

When seeking to establish your network, you gain an awareness of what the other adults in your child's life are like. What are their values and what kind of standards for behavior he or she is likely to observe while your child is present. When you ask people to network you may not always get a positive response. Some adults will not share information with you. Some may give you false information. You may choose not to include particular adults in your network because in your experience they are untrustworthy. Some adults may even attempt to sabotage your discipline. However, most adults will welcome your interest and involvement. They don't want to deal with a misbehaving child any more than you do, but will do so when they believe that corrective action will be taken. Networking is a useful tool in preventing misbehavior. It can also be a useful tool in establishing positive behavior. Think about all the adults in your child's life that can exert influence and model positive behavior. Are there adults of goodwill who can mentor and model success in life for your child? Ask these people to spend time with your child—to encourage and to lift him or her up to the higher places. Children usually respond very well to adults outside their families who take a genuine and healthy interest in them.

Networking Worksheet

To use the skill of networking with the adults in your child's life, you'll need to contact them by phone (or preferably in person). You want to explain to them that you're working on helping your child gain compliance in a particular area (or areas) and would like to enlist their support. Here is a sample script you may want to use.

1. "Hello, I am _____ mother (father). I am calling because I want to have contact with the adults in _____ life. Since you're my child's teacher or (friend's parent, counselor, school nurse, coach, probation officer, caseworker, youth pastor, etc.) I wanted to get to know you."
2. "I want to take a moment to introduce myself and to let you know a few of the rules I/we have for my child since he/she will be in contact with you."
3. State several of your rules. You may want to explain briefly why you have the consequence rule.
4. Ask for the adult's support. Ask him or her to contact you if he or she believes one of the rules has been violated. "You can call, text, or

email me/us at…; home/cell phone numbers are…; these are my/our work hours, and here is how I/we can be contacted at work…"

5. If this is a friend's parents, you may want to add, "I'd like to know some of the rules that you have for your child so that I can monitor and support those rules when the kids are with me."

Network Chain

You can also establish a network chain of concerned adults. Parents and teachers agree to post information for one another on the Internet or through cell phone trees. At times it will be false rumors and fabrications, but the vigilant parent can verify tips about unsupervised parties, adults who hang around school yards, planned fights after school, and other tidbits that the kids may not want you to know. Parents who live in high-crime areas have also banded together to form neighborhood "kid" watches. These parents share what they know about gang, drug, and other criminal activity that might involve their child and agree to help each other.

Network Meeting

Some parents periodically organize informal networking meetings. For ex-ample, at the beginning of the school year, a parent calls a networking meet-ing of her daughter's teacher, school counselor, afterschool community cen-ter worker, and the child's best friend's parents for a short get-together over coffee. Because the child has a history of performing poorly in school with frequent uncompleted assignments, a plan for academic success is discussed. The school counselor agrees to help implement the plan with all of the teachers the child may have. The community center worker agrees to support the plan by tying the amount of time the child can be engaged in recreational activities at the community center with how well she is doing academically. The best friend's parents agree to limit the amount of time the kids can be together and spend in their home if the child has homework to do. They will also have the house monitored by neighbors or electronic equipment to make certain that the kids don't spend the school day hanging out there.

The result of establishing these networks is parents who have moved up their chances of having success in implementing their rules, and who feel supported and encouraged in their parenting. By networking, parents must no longer "go it alone."

TRACKING

People leave behind evidence of their behavior. If you're not sure if your child is engaged in a particular problem behavior, look for the tracks—the physical evidence—that could lead you to the answer. If you think your son is experimenting with stealing—and you have more than casual suspicion— you may search his room, backpack, and clothes, and look for unaccounted for items. You may search the house to see if you find objects there that should not be. You may ask the school to search his locker or desk. You'll track what new items he brings to the house, and demand to see a receipt for each one. If he does not have a receipt, the item goes back to the store or is donated to charity.

Your daughter is failing all of her subjects. You can track her daily academic progress with the Daily Class Assignment Report, coupled with tutoring and networking with her teacher(s).

Your younger son has difficulty not lying. You'll track by going to the source and talking to others involved or contact places to find out the truth anytime that you are suspicious that he is not being truthful about his whereabouts or activities.

MONITORING

Closely related to tracking is the skill of monitoring. Monitoring means reviewing the child's behavior choices and then following up as needed.

- You think your daughter has been disobeying you and jogging in neighborhoods that she does not have permission to be in. You cruise around in the neighborhood to see what she is doing, or monitor her whereabouts using a GPS device on her cell phone.
- Your younger daughter often sneaks her friends into the house when you are not home. You will hire a house sitter to monitor the comings and goings at the house, or install electronic equipment to monitor who is in the house when you are not there.
- Did the kids clean their room? You'll go in and find out.
- Were there any problems when your son stayed overnight at the Jones's house? You'll call the Jones parents and find out.
- Did she lie about Marcie giving her the sweater? You'll check it out with Marcie.

Monitoring allows you to gather the evidence that things are going well or that they are not. A child is considerably less likely to lie or attempt to cover up misbehavior when his or her parent is monitoring consistently.

SUPERVISION

Supervision is a more stringent form of monitoring. It means you need to be there both physically and psychologically for the child to ensure compliance.

- You stand in the doorway while he cleans his room.
- You keep an eye on the clock to ensure that she observes the phone time limit rule.
- You ride the school bus or sit in the class with her because she can't make mature and appropriate decisions for herself when she is alone.
- You have him empty his pockets outside the mall before you take him home.

Preventative Supervision

There is also a type of supervision I call "preventative" as you take physical action to head off misbehavior:

- The child who habitually shoplifts doesn't shop in stores unless he is under the eyeball supervision of a responsible adult.
- The child who cannot be trusted not to make long distance phone calls without permission finds a phone lock.
- The child who eats dessert before dinner finds the dessert locked in the pantry.
- The child who likes to rummage through her parents' bedroom looking for "spare change" finds the bedroom door locked.
- The child who refuses to get out of bed in the morning finds a parent dislodging her from the bed.

This type of discipline is especially effective because it is much easier to *keep* a kid out of trouble in the first place than it is to *get* a kid out of trouble after the fact. How much will most children like and appreciate their parents doing these things? About as well as when they were forced to take baths, pick up their toys, and eat their vegetables when they were younger; in other words not in the least. Which is perfectly okay. Most parents are not going to be too wild about needing to discipline in this way either. The trick for the child is to get mom and dad to lay off by doing what he or she needs to do the first time, and eventually without having to be asked.

ACTIVE CONSEQUENCES AND THE PARENT-CHILD RELATIONSHIP

But aren't active consequences intrusive and likely to make a rebellious kid just that much more rebellious? And doesn't their use serve to erode trust between the parent and child? After all, we don't want to become dictators and have the kids hate us.

Active consequences are designed to be intrusive. Like all manner of discipline, they are meant to be unpleasant and at times embarrassing for the recipient. They teach the child to cultivate the habit of *think before you act, plan before you do*. Think about the consequence that goes with behavior you choose and then plan ahead.

Active consequences can also help stop the rebellious child dead in her tracks by denying her the *opportunity* to misbehave. If you need to use active consequences frequently, it probably means there is very little trust between you and your child already. As your child learns to comply with rules and expectations she is building trust between the two of you. That is why active consequences are so effective when less intrusive forms of discipline are not.

Your child may "hate you" for a time, but that is preferable to his feeling contempt because you cannot influence or control his behavior. The point is not so much whether the active consequence is liked and appreciated, as whether it is effective and gets a response. Indeed it is and it does.

ESCALATING LEVELS OF CONSEQUENCES

Consequence Rule

Rule: Put all dirty clothes in the laundry hamper before washday.
Consequence: Clothes that are not in the hamper will not be washed.

1. Natural consequence: something that happens naturally without parental action: If I don't put my dirty clothes in the hamper on washday, I will have to wear my cleanest pair of dirty underwear.
2. Logical consequence: something arranged beforehand and logically connected to the misbehavior: If I don't get my clothes in the hamper on washday, I will have to do my own laundry.
3. Active consequence: something arranged beforehand and attended to in person by someone in authority: If I don't get my clothes in the hamper on washday, my dad will escort me to my bedroom and hang around until I have picked up all of my dirty clothes, and put them in the hamper (tool used: preventative supervision).

EARNING FREEDOM

So how does a child get a parent to back off and stop employing these embarrassing and annoying and, from some children's perspectives, totally unjust active consequences? How does a parent get a child to go beyond needing active consequences? The answer is simple: by having your child become consistently compliant with the consequence rules and by exercising the freedom that comes with it.

Most children crave one thing more than anything else: *freedom*. They want the freedom to make decisions about the things that affect their lives. They will often tell you that when attempting to strike a deal to do something that they want to do: "Look, you let me do this and I'll have a chance to show you that I am responsible and trustworthy." The formula looks like this: freedom—responsibility—trust. The problem with this preferred formula is the parent gives the incentive first (freedom), followed by the accountability factor (responsibility), followed by the dependability factor (trust).

With responsible kids the formula works just fine. When given the freedom to make their own choices, they assume the responsibility willingly and well. This naturally builds a trust bond between the parent and the child. The result is we can extend even more freedom to the child. With the semi-responsible and irresponsible child we will have a problem putting the formula into effect.

The semi-responsible child will consistently have difficulty handling her freedom in one or two areas of concern. She does her chores and homework consistently. She attends school regularly. But she is stealing money and sometimes tobacco from the house and giving and using it with her friends. When asked, she has lied about it.

The irresponsible child has difficulty handling her freedom in most areas of concern. She does her chores or homework only when she is prodded into doing them, and then she does the bare minimum. She skips classes regularly. She consistently steals money, alcohol, and tobacco from the house, which she shares with her friends and peers, and when asked, routinely lies about it.

With semi-responsible and irresponsible kids like these, the formula works better this way: trust—responsibility—freedom. The child earns trust by becoming consistently compliant with rules and expectations. She demonstrates responsibility by accepting the consequences that go with the rules. She demonstrates responsibility by being consistently trustworthy in little things too: doing her chores and homework without having to be pushed or prodded, getting to bed on time, getting up in the morning, being home at the proper time, and not arguing or being deliberately irritating. She earns freedom by demonstrating that she can handle the freedom she is given.

By doing these things consistently, your child is taking the initiative to be responsible. She is rightly earning freedom—a small amount of freedom at first, with increasingly more freedom as she demonstrates more responsible and trustworthy behavior.

Many kids older than nine or so have a good deal of personal freedom. They can come and go, do things with their friends, do their homework and chores when they choose to, have special privileges, and make most of their own age-appropriate decisions within reason. These children needed to earn their freedom, based upon their demonstrated level of trustworthy and responsible behavior. They don't have total freedom—no one does—and the parents are aware of what is happening in their lives and the decisions they are making. This is the kind of freedom that families should strive for.

When the wanted behavior is consistently in place, discontinue using the consequence. You may require a one-time use of the consequence—be it the natural, logical, or active consequence—or it may take months of consistent use, but the end will come. Afterwards, continue to use positive rewards to reinforce the occurrence of the new positive behavior. Through your use of consequences—negative consequences for misbehavior, and positive consequences for positive behavior—your child is in a position to get what he wants, not just from you, but from other adult authority figures as well. How? By demonstrating that he is trustworthy with the freedom he does have. The more trustworthy he is the more freedom he has; the less trustworthy, the less freedom.

Tell your child, "You get just as much freedom as you demonstrate you can handle successfully." Is this not the same standard you used when your child was even younger? When did you decide they no longer needed a babysitter? When could she go to the park, or stay overnight at a friend's house, or even go on her first long trip? For most parents, it was when their children demonstrated by the yardstick for their behavior that they could handle the situation.

In complying with consequence rules, *children* control the amount, degree, and kind of freedom that they earn in the discipline plan. You can wait for your kids to learn to "be more responsible," or you can place the weight of their personal accountability squarely on their own shoulders.

- You can choose any elective course you like—you just can't choose to fail.
- You can consume any healthy substance you like—but not tobacco or illegal drugs.
- You can stay out as long as you like—as long as you're home before the scheduled time.

What do you have when you have a child who consistently makes the choice to pass all of his subjects, not use tobacco/illegal drugs, and be home by a set time? A kid who has a great deal more personal freedom that he otherwise would have based upon his behavior; a child who is moving toward becoming a self-directed and self-motivated person who requires very little active parental discipline. This is exactly what we want.

ACTIVE CONSEQUENCES NEEDED

Johnny

Johnny was still in bed when his mother called him for the fourth time. He had been up all night texting his friends and playing Evil Unchained and he didn't get to sleep until he didn't know when. He drank two of the Zipper energy drinks to stay awake and took three—or was it four?—of those little brown pills that DJ had given him. He got a good buzz off of them and then he crashed when the sun came up. It was righteous. Johnny was tired and had absolutely no intention of going to school today. His mother was just as adamant that Johnny would get out of bed and go to school.

"Johnny! I'm going to be late for work. Now come on, honey, get out of bed. It's the first day of 6th grade! Middle school! You don't want to miss that."

Johnny pulled the blanket under his chin.

"Johnny!"

"What!?"

"You know what. Get out of bed right now."

"I'm sick."

"You're not sick. You stayed up all blessed night playing that game and texting your friends."

"I went to bed when I was supposed to; you don't know," Johnny lied. "And I'm not going to school today."

"John—knee!" the mother whined. "It's the first day of school. You don't want to miss that. C'mon, summer is over."

"I don't care. School is boring and all the teachers are a bunch of meatheads."

"You want to fail all of your subjects again?"

"Oh, so I'm going to fail. I'm just a total failure."

"I didn't say that."

"But that's what you meant."

"What am I going to do with you? Johnny, I love you. But if you don't stop playing video games in your room all day and night, and stop drinking those speed drinks—yes, I found the empties. . . ."

"Oh, so now I am a total loser and a drug addict!"

"No . . . . It's those damn friends of yours. DJ gets you to do—"

"Oh, so now I don't have a brain. My friends do all of my thinking for me!"

"Johnny . . . Fine. You do what you want today. I'll write you an excuse. Just please go to school tomorrow."

"I will. Just quit worrying about me, okay? Everything is fine."

"Okay. Just don't be mad, okay?"

"I'm not, Mom. Love you."

"Love you too, honey."

Johnny's mother left for work confident that she had gotten through to Johnny about the importance of regular school attendance and not staying up late. Johnny went back to sleep and slept most of the day. Late that afternoon he resumed playing Evil Unchained, texting his friends, and drinking Zipper with DJ's little brown pills in order to stay awake. Johnny did not attend school for the rest of the week, or the next week. When Johnny's school principal called to inquire about his absence from school, his mother assured him that Johnny had been "sick" and would return to school "soon."

David

David liked to hit people. Well, not just anybody. Mostly it was just little kids. They deserved it; they were annoying, and they kept getting in his way. You had to teach them who was running the show and that there was a price to pay if they didn't do what he wanted. David did feel a little bit bad about taking their allowance and lunch money—he didn't really need the money—but hey, if their stupid parents were dumb enough to give them money, then they ought to lose it. At least that was the way that Christopher said it. Christopher was a "big" kid. He went to the high school. He was mean, and you didn't cross him—you just gave him half of the money. David was glad he was Christopher's friend. He'd seen Christopher beat up a lot of people and he didn't want to be included.

David was a little worried about his parents finding out about his pushing around the little kids. He told them to keep their traps shut or they'd pay a lot more than money. He also sent the ones with cell phones intimidating text messages. So far the school didn't know anything about it, and if they did they couldn't prove it, right? David was putting away his weekly cash when his dad walked through the front door.

"Hey, guy."

"Hi Dad."

David's father was exhausted after an eleven-hour workday. He was looking at another one just like it tomorrow.

"You want to eat out?"

"Mom's not home yet," David said.

"She won't be for another hour. She said go ahead."

"Let's do it."

"You got all your chores done?"

"Yeah."

"Schoolwork?"

"Yeah."

"Anything new?"

"Nope."

"Cool. Let's do the steak place."

David's father left the house that evening feeling assured that he knew everything of importance in his son's life. David was glad that evening that he had such good parents. All such goodwill evaporated the following week when David was arrested for assault and menacing by the school resource officer. David was found at the bus stop with a third grader's lunch money in hand and the bloodied child lying on the ground. David told the officer that he had "found" the money and that the child had stepped on his foot. David's parents were humiliated and appalled when they picked up their ten-year-old son at the police station.

Leah

Leah was talking to her friend on the phone when her grandmother came into the living room.

"Leah, get off the phone."

"What?"

"You said that you'd pick up the living room an hour ago, and you're still talking. Come on, girl."

Leah's grandmother began to pick up the clothes on the floor.

"I'll call you back," Leah said to her friend and hung up. "Geez, Grandma, that's embarrassing when I'm on the phone like that."

Leah's grandmother began to stack the newspapers.

"Come and help me," she said.

Leah moved empty soda cans from one end of the couch to the other.

"Have you fed Lucky yet?"

"Not yet. You told me to clean up the living room. I've been doing my homework."

Leah pointed to the undisturbed pile of books next to the couch.

"She's your dog, you know," Leah's grandmother said.

Leah's grandmother got out the vacuum cleaner and began to sweep. Leah picked up three empty soda cans and slowly walked in to the kitchen. She dropped the cans into the recycling bin and then walked extra slowly back into the living room. Her grandmother was rewinding the cord on the vacuum cleaner.

"There," she said brightly. "Now that wasn't so bad."

Leah agreed that it wasn't so bad. She picked up the phone to call her friend. The homework was never done that evening because Leah "didn't have time." She took an F on her assignment. The dog was not fed until late that night when Leah's grandmother got tired of listening to the animal howl.

ACTIVE CONSEQUENCES AT WORK

Johnny

Johnny's mother was informed by the school that they had no recourse but to drop him from enrollment because he was not in school. Further, they would be referring the mother for legal sanctions because she had not made an effort to get Johnny to school. They offered one more day. In desperation, Johnny's mother turned to her brother for help.

Uncle Don said that he had read the first *Decisive Parenting* book and knew he could help. Uncle Don came to the house the next morning and rousted a sleeping Johnny from his bed. Johnny was shocked and angry. Uncle Don told him, "You have ten minutes to be ready to go to school. I will drive you. If you refuse to go into the school a security guard and I will escort you to class and I will sit with you the entire day." Once at school, Johnny decided it was to his advantage to go to class.

While Johnny was at school the mother and Uncle Don searched Johnny's bedroom. They confiscated all of his electronic equipment, found and destroyed the "little brown pills," and emptied all of Johnny's Zipper drinks down the drain. When Johnny came home from school he was told that his substance abusing days were over and shown a list of consequence rules and how he could earn back his electronic gadgets, one at a time. He was asked for his input. He had none.

Johnny was told that Uncle Don was a phone call away and would repeat the morning's consequences if Johnny chose to have him do so. Johnny reluctantly agreed to comply.

Three weeks into the discipline plan Johnny attended school and did his assignments every day but one—which resulted in an early morning visit from Uncle Don. He grumbled and complained, but was compliant. Then one day Uncle Don picked up Johnny from school and told him he had a "surprise" for him. Uncle Don took Johnny out to an athletic field where a group of boys his age were practicing a game called lacrosse. Johnny had never heard of lacrosse but was interested After a time he asked if he could try to play and was shown the basics by the coach. Johnny loved lacrosse and wanted to play. Johnny's mother agreed to allow him to practice and play on the lacrosse team as long as his attendance and grades were satisfactory with no evidence of drug use. Johnny became so enamored with lacrosse and enjoying his success in school that he only played video games once in a great while. His friendship with DJ the drug dealer faded.

David

David appeared in juvenile court with his parents. The judge ordered that David be assigned a juvenile probation officer and a court counselor that he would meet with weekly. David had to complete an accountability contract with the juvenile court. He was required to successfully complete an anti-bullying group at the Boys and Girls Club. He was also ordered to pay restitution to his victims and to make formal apologies. David's parents required that he perform community service as well as extra chores around the house and paid him the minimum wage which was given in compensation to his victims. An adult mentor at the school supervised David's behavior on the playground and at the bus stop. David's parents networked with all the adults in his life and consistently monitored where he was, who he was with, and what he was doing. David never saw Christopher again. David's parents praised his continuing efforts. He quickly gave up his bullying ways.

Leah

Leah's grandmother insisted that they establish some consequence rules for Leah's problem behaviors. At first Leah refused to participate in rule construction. Leah's grandmother said she would proceed without her. When Leah saw the first draft of the rules and consequences, she decided that they were too harsh and punitive and then eagerly joined in the second round of rule construction.

Leah was put on a daily schedule for chore and homework completion. Leah's grandmother set up a point chart for Leah to earn positive consequences and freedom in exchange for doing chores and homework to a high standard. Leah's grandmother monitored consistently and did not help her do her work. After a slow start, and within three weeks, Leah was doing her homework and chores about 60 percent of the time without her grandmother's prodding. Within six weeks Leah was doing all of her school assignments and chores every day with no reminders. Her grades shot up and she and her grandmother found that each had more quality free time to do as they pleased.

Chapter Five

Level Systems, Point Economies, and Contracts

The two most common discipline practices parents use with children are grounding and taking away privileges. If these discipline methods work consistently for you, well and good. If they do not—if, for example, your child makes your life miserable for the two weeks he is off his privileges and in the house—you may need more skills to choose from.

Three skills commonly used in effective juvenile programs that can be adapted to home use are:

- Level Systems—the child earns privileges and freedom at different behavior levels
- Point Economies—the child earns points that he can exchange for privileges and desires
- Contracts—the child and parent make voluntary formal agreements

Use of these skills requires the same level of active parental involvement as the active consequence covered in chapter 4. Likewise, they are extremely effective with *all* children, but can be especially useful with difficult children. You can also use all three skills simultaneously depending on the issue at hand.

LEVEL SYSTEMS

In most successful juvenile programs, there is a behavioral level system in place. Children generally start out with a low level of freedom and privilege and work their way up through the system to a maximum level of privilege and freedom.

Something akin to this system can be used at home as an *alternative* to grounding and taking away privileges. Level systems do not work well all the time. However, for serious instances of misbehavior, you may want to give them a try.

When your child has engaged in some serious misbehavior, such as re-peatedly hitting or injuring a sibling or another child, or vandalizing or destroying property, and you wish to ground him for a time, consider using a level system such as the one illustrated below.

Level I, Forty-Eight Hours

House restriction for forty-eight hours. _____ must stay in the house (unless attending school). There are no privileges at this level. _____ may not talk/text on the phone, watch TV, play the radio or stereo, use the computer for other than schoolwork, play video games, or have contact with friends. _____ will complete all school assign-ments and assigned chores without complaint and with parental verification. _____ will not argue or complain about freedom restrictions.

Forty-eight hours of compliant behavior will result in a move to level II status at the parent's discretion.

Level II, Forty-Eight Hours

Must stay in the house or on the immediate property (unless attending school). Can watch TV and make one fifteen-minute phone call(s) per day _____ can participate in family outings as long as at least one of the parents is present. _____ will complete all school assignments and assigned chores without complaint and with parental verifi-cation.

Forty-eight hours of compliant behavior will result in a move to level III status at the parent's discretion.

Level III, Twenty-Four Hours

_____ has all of the privileges of Level II. In addition, _____ can visit a friend or have a friend visit the house for one hour with parental permission. Further, _____ can watch TV, talk/text on the phone, play the radio or stereo, play video games, or use the computer to whatever level parents feel is appropriate. _____ will complete all school assignments and assigned chores with parental ver-ification.

Twenty-four hours of compliant behavior will result in a move to level IV status at the parent's discretion.

Level IV, Twenty-Four Hours

_____ has all of the privileges of Level III. _____ can leave the house with parental permission for a specified period of time for an approved activity, with a required phone call when he/she arrives at the destination. At Level IV, parents may require a formal problem-solving meeting with _____ in order to come to an agreement about how to prevent a recurrence of the problem behavior that led to the use of the level system.

Twenty-four hours of compliant behavior will result in the removal of the level system restrictions.

Any of the following behaviors will result in a drop in level status as follows:

- Verbal abuse: Level I for twenty-four hours
- Physical threats or abuse: Level I for forty-eight hours
- Lying: Level I for twenty-four hours
- Stealing: Level decreased to former level for twenty-four hours plus school/parent/store contact with any needed action
- Drug or alcohol use: Level I for seven days plus any needed evaluation/treatment follow-up
- Persistent negative attitude and behavior: Drop to the former level.
- Running away or being gone without permission: three hours of Level I for every hour gone without permission.
- Other: To be arranged.

This six-day level system is usually more effective and consistent than a typical grounding. In conventional restrictions, a child must only "be there" and "do time" in order to get off grounding. He need not demonstrate any change in behavior or outlook. There are no expectations for trustworthy, responsible behavior, and no method to measure it.

In a level system, the *child* controls the degree of freedom and privilege she receives. She must demonstrate she is trustworthy and responsible with the personal freedom she does earn. Further, a child can drop a level or more for choosing noncompliance. This is a logical consequence for failure to follow the terms of the previous level.

Permanent Level System

What about using a level system with a more permanent structure? You certainly can. The permanent level system is dependent upon the age and maturity of the child.

Here is how it works. You first specify your child's rules and responsibilities. You also specify the privileges your child currently enjoys. For every instance of breaking a rule, or for failure to follow through on a responsibility, he loses one privilege. If he follows all of the rules and meets all of the responsibilities, he gets to keep and use all of his privileges. He may earn extra or special privileges with the use of a point system (discussed in a later section of this chapter).

When should the permanent level system be changed? When the rules and expectations change, or when the maturity level of the child requires a different set of privileges. I suggest you review the program with your child at least twice a year, and make adjustments accordingly. Here are examples for a four-year-old and for a twelve-year old.

Rules and expectations for Clint:

1. Be out of bed, dress yourself, comb your hair, brush your teeth, and be ready for breakfast by 7:30 in the morning time.
2. Have your backpack ready to go with you to daycare by 8:00 in the morning time.
3. Be ready to go home from daycare when Mommy or Daddy comes to pick you up.
4. Be ready to have your bath, pajamas on, and your teeth brushed by 8:30 at night.

Now, of course, this may sound like a lot for a four-year-old child (especially for one who can't read or tell time); indeed it is. But all of these behavioral expectations occur in Clint's life, so why not make them part of his daily routine? An easy way to help Clint understand what is expected of him is to make a poster with photographs of Clint *doing* each behavior. Here is little Clint getting out of bed, getting dressed, combing his hair, brushing his teeth, sitting at the breakfast table, putting his favorite toys in his backpack, and so on. Decorate the poster and place it in the child's room at eye level. Have the child practice the routine until it is established.

Routine privileges for Clint:

1. Clint can play or watch TV until his bedtime routine at 8:00 in the nighttime.
2. Clint can have Mommy or Daddy read him a story before he goes to sleep in the nighttime.

3. Clint can choose an "outing" with Mommy, Daddy or both once a week.
4. Clint can have a play date with one of his friends once a week.

Clint, like most four-year-olds, likes to make choices for himself. He can be resistive at times to his parents' directions and wind up in a power struggle when he wants to make his own choices and the parents want the opposite. So how did Clint do the first week of his permanent level system?

Because Clint's parents were patient and praised him while he learned the new routine, Clint was considerably less resistive to his parents' expectations for him; but on occasion when he did refuse his parents followed through consistently and subtracted one of his privileges. Clint learned that he was on a *schedule* and that the schedule would not vary; he accepted that he was being a "big boy" and was doing things that gave him a sense of control. He also realized that he was more likely to be given the privileges that were his because he had *earned* them.

In the months following, there were occasional times when Clint would be resistive to what his parents wanted—he didn't want to go to bed at the scheduled time, he didn't want to brush his teeth that morning. But when his parents redirected him to follow *his* schedule he usually quickly complied. As Clint grew older, his list of rules and expectations and desired rewards were modified a bit, but with continued good success.

Here is an example for twelve-year-old Tamara.

Rules and expectations for Tamara:

1. Pass all of your current class assignments with a letter grade of C or higher.
2. Be home for the night by 6:00 every weeknight.
3. Complete one major assigned chore once a week and all daily chores.
4. Never use obscene language or yell at anyone in the family.

Routine privileges for Tamara:

1. Can make (or receive) up to three ten-minute phone calls an evening.
2. Can stay up until 10:00 on school nights and until 11:00 on Friday and Saturday nights.
3. Can visit friends (or have them over) until 6:00 on school nights and until 10:30 on Friday and Saturday nights.
4. Can be allowed to go to the movies, the mall, religious services, school functions, parties or other approved activities during the day and under supervision at night.

So how did Tamara do on the first week of the permanent level system? Her parents tracked her progress using the Rules Tracking Guide. She followed through successfully on rules 1, 2, and 3, but on Thursday she got into a screaming match with her brother over the use of the computer and called him several unprintable names. She lost all of her computer privileges for the day. On Friday she did not complete her major chore, which was to gather and load all of the towels, bed sheets, and white linen into the washing machine and then the dryer. She lost the chance to spend the evening at her friend's house and came in for the night at 6:00. She spent the evening completing her laundry chore. However, Tamara did earn all of her other specified privileges for the week. The next week she avoided the problems of the first week and earned all of her privileges.

Tamara's seventeen-year-old sister has a permanent level system of her own. Her list of rules and expectations is different because she has different behaviors she is working on. Likewise, her list of routine privileges is different from Tamara's based upon her age and level of maturity. The older sister has a later bedtime, can engage in some activities at night without supervision, and has more freedom with friends and choices. As Tamara gets older and demonstrates more ability to make appropriate choices for herself, she too should be on a permanent level system with more freedom.

In this system of checks and balances, your child still has all of his or her *needs* met unconditionally: food, clothing, shelter, personal items, education, and expressions of love. At least some of his or her *wants* are also met. In order to secure special privileges beyond the routine ones, or things that are especially wanted, you can couple the use of the permanent level system with the point economy—which will be explained shortly. In order to increase its effectiveness, be sure to offer frequent praise and encouragement on how well the kid is doing on her system.

Finally you can use the shorthand version of the level system, if you prefer. This version may prove especially useful for the generally compliant child. Your child is put on restriction for a week or a day for some misbehavior or rule infraction. However, she still must prove that she is trustworthy and responsible.

Linda, who is generally a trustworthy kid, has been in the house for three days now because she went up to the store to buy milk and a loaf of bread. But instead she was talked into giving the money to her new friend so they could buy cigarettes. Linda came wandering in two hours past dinnertime, reeking of tobacco.

Linda realizes that she did something really stupid and has been apologetic. She has finished her time on grounding, but now will be given only a small amount of freedom out of the house. Today she gets to go out at 4:00 pm, and she has to be back by 4:30 pm. If Linda handles that well she gets another half hour the next day, and the next. Linda then earns an hour, an hour and a half, and so forth, with no evidence of wrongdoing. Finally, by the end of the week Linda is back to the level of freedom out of the house she once enjoyed. What if Linda blows it? Then she goes back to the last level of freedom where she was successful.

The same idea holds true if you are restoring privileges after a short grounding. Your child gets his TV privileges back today, his phone privileges back tomorrow, and his friend visits the next day depending on how he did today. The key is that at each step in the process, your child must now demonstrate he is trustworthy and responsible by making good choices.

POINT ECONOMIES

The idea behind a point economy is simple: your child earns points based upon his behavior and the points are exchanged for privileges. The more points he earns, the more privileges he earns.

For example, you want your son to make his bed upon rising and have his bedroom in order before he leaves for school. You have a consequence rule about making the bed and keeping the room clean: if he doesn't do it on his own, you stand in the doorway while he does the chore.

Now you add an incentive if he does the chore by awarding a set number of points for chore completion. Your child complies with the rule, avoids a consequence, and earns an incentive. The result is that you are much more likely to see the behavior change you want in a short time. Point economies work best when you construct them with your child. The child's input regarding the incentive he would like to earn helps ensure success. Encourage your child to keep a parallel point chart so they can be aware of how they are doing during the day and week. Give extra points for keeping an accurate log.

You can establish point economies for:

- Routine and expected behaviors, such as chores, school attendance, and homework completion.
- Problem behavior you want to see eliminated such as arguing with parents, backtalk, bullying, and sibling fighting.
- Behaviors you want to see more of, such as asking for help with homework, actively seeking to help others, speaking to others respectfully, learning about and performing manners, and others.

You can occasionally give spontaneous points for behavior you liked as well. For example, your sons played video games for two hours without any name calling—10 points; your daughter didn't interrupt and argue while you were on the phone during your business call—10 points; your older daughter came right home and started on her afternoon chores—10 points.

Children like the point economy because they can see a clear benefit to themselves. They are complying with family rules, avoiding unpleasant consequences, and earning something that they want. Parents like the point economy because it increases child compliance, rewards wanted behavior that is likely to be repeated, and avoids conflict.

To use a point economy effectively, link the giving of points with praise and acknowledgment. Be strict about the giving of points: either your child has performed the behavior and has earned the points, or she has not. Don't give half or quarter points, and don't give points for behavior that has not yet occurred. For each behavior, it is best to use a number such as 10. It is confusing and burdensome to give two points for this and seven points for that. Do not subtract points for noncompliance. Once the points are earned they are earned; no behavior, no points.

Points need to be exchanged for privileges or incentives within a short time—that day or within a week. Just as the department store offers a two-for-one sale for a week's time, so should the incentive be relatively small and close in time to when the desired behavior occurs. Make a chart like the ones below of the behavior change you desire, a description of what you want to see, when it is supposed to happen, how many points it is worth, and if it was earned.

Here are two examples. This chart is for Monday through Friday. There are 50 possible points each day.

Table 5.1. Point Chart for Jake

Behavior	Description	Deadline	Points Earned (0 or 10)
Up on time	Out of bed and bed made, showered, dressed, teeth brushed, hair combed	6:45 am	10
School on time	Catch the bus; arrive at all classes on time	7:00 am–2:20 pm	10
Daily Class Assignment Report	Complete the DCAR; have each teacher sign it; bring it home to parents	3:00 pm	10
Homework	Complete all daily assignments when due		10
Daily chores	Complete all assigned chores		10

If Jake earns the total 50 points for the day, he may have:

- One additional hour on the computer
- Fifteen additional minutes on his cell phone

If Jake earns at least 220 of the 250 points possible for the week, he may have:

- The chance to be out with his friends on Friday or Saturday night in an approved activity
- A movie pass
- $10

If Rene earns 30 points most days and 40 points on Monday and Thursday, she may have:

- Social network access on her computer for that day
- A friend over or visit a friend until dinner time

If Rene earns at least 200 of the 230 points possible for the week, Rene may have:

- The chance to be out with friends on Friday night or Saturday in an approved setting
- $20 in art supplies

Table 5.2.   Point Chart for Rene

Behavior	Description	Timeline	Points Earned (0 or 10)
Stealing	Having a receipt for every item in her possession that is questioned	Parent review seven days a week	10
Lying	Telling the truth when asked	Parent review seven days a week	10
Check-in	Coming home on schedule; returning phone call on her cell phone within five minutes	Parent review seven days a week	10
Homework	Complete all daily assignments when due		10
Chores	Preparing and cooking dinner	Monday and Thursday	10

- A weekly video rental

Ways Children Can Earn Extra Points

- Say please and thank you in a pleasant tone and show your appreciation in other ways.
- Offer to help when you see that others need it.
- Ask for help instead of becoming frustrated and angry.
- Say something positive to someone or give a compliment.
- Follow-through with requests the first time you're asked.
- Take responsibility for behavior choices by acknowledging mistakes.
- Do chores and homework without being reminded.
- Communicate with parents using problem-solving skills.
- Don't argue.
- Obey all rules.
- Do acts of kindness.

CONTRACTS

A contract is a formal agreement between two or more people as to what each will do to fulfill the terms of the contract. A contract says if something takes place, something else will happen as a result of that both parties have agreed to, or understand will happen.

Contracts are different for the rules and consequences than use of the discipline plan. With the contract you and your child come to an agreement each makes *voluntarily*.

Contracts do not work well with all kids. Children who are vain and impulsive often do not do well with contracts, but some do. Further, kids that are enmeshed with negative friends, or deeply involved in delinquency, will often not do well with contracts, but some do quite well if the contracts are applied consistently. If you think you might need help, most therapists are familiar with contracting, and you may wish to enlist the help of one in devising a contract. The best advice is to try out a *small* short-term contract and monitor how well it works for you. If you have good success, try a larger, long-term contract.

Further, just like with rules, have a small number of contracts. You don't want to contract for every behavior that your child is capable of doing.

There are at least three different kinds of contracts you can use to formalize agreements between you and your child. There are (1) "if/then" contracts (sometimes called "contingency contracts"), (2) "in-exchange-for" contracts (sometimes called "quid pro quo contracts"), and (3) "good faith" contracts.

All three contracts involve contingencies and consequences, but they work in different ways.

If/Then Contracts

If/Then contracts can be written or oral. They have two parts, the specified behavior, (the contingency) if . . . , and the consequence, then . . . , which is dependent on the contingency. I might make oral if/then contracts like these with my kids:

- "Kayla, if you'll sweep out the garage, and neatly stack all of the boxes (the contingency), I'll pay you five dollars" (the consequence).
- "Andrea, when you've finished the dishes (the contingency) you can go to the movies with Susan" (the consequence).
- "Jeff, if you come straight home from school every day this week and check in (the contingency), then I'll lift the rest of your grounding (the consequence), and you can go to the dance."

The contract must be worded so that both parties can see a clear connection between the specified behavior and the consequence: if *this* happens, *that* will happen; when *that* occurs, *this* will occur. But the contract is only as good as the will of both parties to follow it.

A written contract is best for longer term events, or events that could happen more than once. It also has the advantage of being written and signed with a copy to each party, which helps prevent arguments later over exactly what the contract specified. It can be worded just as an oral contract is.

You may have a written if/then contract for sibling fighting, chores, homework, using the bicycle, or any number of other behaviors. You can write the contract during a meeting with the entire family.

In-Exchange-For Contracts

In-Exchange-For contracts are those in which the behavior of one person is dependent on that of another. For example, you may agree to do your child's dinner dishes chore for one night in exchange for the child doing your garbage chore the next night. Or you may agree to drive your kids to the mall and give them a little spending money, if they agree to make dinner that night. You can also have a written In-Exchange-For contracts. You might agree to pay the tuition for your kid to attend equestrian camp this summer, if she agrees to provide babysitting for her little sister for three months.

With the In-Exchange-For contracts you've agreed to make an exchange of behaviors that are predicated on the willingness of each person to strike a bargain. "You get what you want, I get what I want." But neither party gets what they want if one party doesn't live up to the agreement. Here are some examples:

- In exchange for weekly cleaning her room to an agreed upon standard, Mary will earn the privilege to hang one wall poster in her room (at her own expense).
- In exchange for meeting for two hours a week with his math tutor, Joel will earn a movie pass. When he completes all of his math assignments for the week, Joel will earn a second movie pass he can use to take a friend to the movies.
- For every day that Cassandra does not talk back to her parents, she can place two fifteen-minute phone calls to her friends.

Good Faith Contracts

Finally, there is the good faith contract, in which the behavior of one person is *independent* of that of another. You are simply saying this is what I want or I intend to do, and are consulting with others (parents) and listening to any objections.

- Your child can do as she pleases when she has completed all of her homework and chores.
- Your son can have a sleepover at the house and will pay all of the expenses.
- Your daughter will go on the ski trip and will wrap her sprained ankle.

You can make a good faith contract with yourself that is not contingent on anyone else's behavior. You can have a written contract with yourself that you'll practice one of the new skills you're learning for one month. As an incentive, you will see a movie at the theatre. Or you can make a good faith contract to get out of bed on Friday, Saturday, or Sunday morning, get ready for religious services, and ask the kids to come along. As an incentive, you'll take yourself—and anyone who comes along—out for breakfast. Or you can make a contract with yourself to practice anger management skills for a month when the kids upset you. If you're successful treat yourself to a round of golf.

Extending the idea of the good faith contract, you can write a contract involving you and your spouse. This contract is an agreement that pledges support for the other person. You simply say that you agree to the best of your ability to help the other parent in some specific ways. For example, you can write: "I will seek not to contradict you when you are giving a directive to the kids; I will compliment you on your using new parenting skills; comment approvingly on the progress I see the family is making; console you during setbacks; keep my doubts to myself; and strive to maintain a positive attitude." The incentive here is having a happier and healthier relationship with your parenting partner, as well as greater likelihood of parenting success.

Contracts are very useful tools you can use to increase your odds of achieving behavior change with your child. Contracts are also tools you may find useful in building bridges between you and your child, as well as between you and your best intentions.

CONTRACT EXAMPLES

The Jones family has three children: nine-year-old Sara, eleven-year-old Jeff, and twelve-year-old Kimberly. The Jones parents wish to write a contract for each of the kids to address certain behaviors. Here are the Jones family contracts.

For the Jones Family

If/Then Contract

Date: December 5, 20 ___
Date for Review: February 2, 20 ___
Contracted behavior: regular attendance and consistent effort in dance classes.
Description of requirements: Sara Jones agrees to the terms of this contract between her and her parents.

1. Attend every scheduled dance class
2. Follow through with all directions of the teacher
3. Be responsible for bringing her dance clothes and equipment to each class
4. Be cooperative with all students in the class
5. Practice her assigned dance steps in between classes
6. Maintain her chore completion schedule at home
7. Maintain a B grade point average in school in order to retain her dance class privileges

Contingencies:

1. If Sara violates any of the conditions set forth above, then the parents will require a problem-solving meeting with Sara and, if necessary, the dance teacher.

2. If Sara cannot resolve the problem in the next week, then Sara will be placed on restriction from attending dance classes for one week or possibly be withdrawn from dance class.
3. If Sara attends all her dance classes on time, with her equipment, and makes a good effort in class, the parents agree to continue to pay for all of Sara's classes and to attend her practices and recitals with enthusiastic support.

Child's signature: <u>Sara Jones</u>
Parent's signature: <u>Catherine Jones</u>
Parent's signature: <u>Bill Jones</u>

In-Exchange-For Contract for Jeff, Eleven Years Old

Date: January 1, 20____
Date for review: March 15, 20____
Contracted behavior: <u>anger management</u>
Description:

1. Jeff Jones agrees to attend weekly therapy sessions with his therapist, Dr. Phillip Smith.
2. Jeff agrees to be forthcoming with Dr. Smith, and to complete any homework assignments for anger management.
3. Jeff agrees to participate in a monthly family therapy session with the therapist.
4. Dr. Smith will be the judge of whether Jeff is fully participating in therapy.

Contingencies:

1. In exchange for Jeff attending all weekly sessions and participating fully in therapy as judged by Dr. Smith, during the next 6 weeks, he will earn the chance to try out for the middle school wrestling team. His parents agree to purchase Jeff's wrestling equipment, attend all of his meets, and enthusiastically support the progress he is making in therapy and on the wrestling team.

Child's signature: <u>Jeff Jones</u>
Parent's signature: <u>Catherine Jones</u>
Parent's signature: <u>Bill Jones</u>

Good Faith Contract

Date: May 10, 20____

Date for review: September 1, 20____
Contracted behavior: <u>notification of parties</u>
Description:

1. I, Kimberly Jones, agree to give my parents forty-eight hours' notice if I wish to attend a party.
2. I will provide my parents with the names, addresses, and phone numbers of the people who are hosting the party.
3. I agree that my parents can make contact with the hosts to go over the details before giving consent for me to attend the party.

Child's signature: <u>Kimberly Jones</u>
Parent's signature: <u>Catherine Jones</u>
Parent's signature: <u>Bill Jones</u>

USING CONTRACTS AND INCENTIVES TOGETHER

To use larger rewards over a longer period of time, keep a log of all the points your child has earned each week over the last 4 months. If the average is 90–100 percent of possible points your child has earned, then award a "bonus" reward; if an average of 80–89 percent of possible points, a slightly less desirable reward. The same idea if 70–79 percent of points are earned. Do not give anything for compliance under 70 percent. Use an if/then contract to specify the reward and percentage of points to be earned.

For example, Isaiah has a rate of 90 percent compliance over the last four months. He has contracted to go on a camping trip with his uncle for four days. If Isaiah had a rate of 80 percent, then the camping trip would be cut back to three days; with 70 percent compliance, it would be two days.

A sleepover for your child at the house would be for this many hours, guests, and activities, depending on the percentage of points earned. More points will get the child more hours, guests, and activities; fewer points results in fewer hours, guests, and activities. The bonus incentives you reward should be for more expensive or elaborate rewards for consistent compliance—but nothing extravagant. Examples might include a desired item, event tickets, or special trips, activities, or privileges. Offer these incentives once every four months, three times a year.

Chapter Six

Distraction/Diversion, Ignoring, Time-Out, Shaping, and Punishments That You Should Never Use

This chapter is about using discipline skills that are especially useful with children under age two and ages three to five. Distraction/diversion, ignoring, and time-out are all common behavioral techniques that are widely used by parents of young children.

DIVERSION/DISTRACTION

You have probably used the distraction/diversion technique to stop a baby's unwanted behavior—even if you didn't know that parenting "experts" call it that. A baby crawls toward the lamp or some desirable, easily breakable shiny object. You intercept and divert the little explorer by scooping him up in your arms and sitting between him and the object of fascination. After sitting the baby down, if he makes a beeline to the prohibited object you repeat the process. If he fusses or cries you distract his attention by offering a favorite toy or less desirable—but safe—object to have and to hold. After a number of trials, the baby learns that certain behavior choices will not be allowed and will be immediately stopped, so there is no point in attempting to have his way.

   This technique works well for most babies. But some babies and toddlers are more strong-willed than others, and it requires repetition and patience on the parent's part to be successful. If you're consistent, it *will* work. And, it is usually the first discipline a child experiences so it lays the foundation for other successful discipline techniques.

IGNORING

Ignoring unwanted or coercive behavior from a toddler or young child can be done, though it's not always pleasant. The idea is that when young children protest and cry, "I don't *wanna* take a bath!" "No peas for Jamie!" "He did it too!" "Pleazzzze, let me drive the car!"—you get the idea—you turn your gaze away from them and don't interact until the obnoxious behavior ceases. This technique works because if you plead, argue, demand, yell, whine—or give in—you are reinforcing the child's negative behavior by playing along with it and giving it undue attention. It also greatly increases the likelihood of children repeating the same behavior. Your "no" word needs to be the last word on the subject. When the child stops the behavior, you return your gaze and attention and go about the business of settling the matter.

TIME-OUT

When the concept of time-out was first introduced by behavioral psychologists, it was called "time-out from positive reinforcement." Positive reinforcement involves providing the child with consistent positive attention and interaction. If the child misbehaves this positive parental interaction is briefly taken away; in fact, all activity is briefly taken away. The fun stops and the penalty for bad behavior commences. However, when time-out is used correctly, it can be a very effective discipline tool for parents of young children.

Preparing the Child for Time-Out

By the time a child is a two-year-old they are old enough to understand the purpose of time-out. In addition to simply interrupting an unacceptable behavior, you are now directing the child to use a time-out space to regain control of their behavior, and to think about what misbehavior resulted in their losing their positive time.

To use time-out this is what you do:

1. Before you use time-out for the first time, find a small chair and place it in a safe but boring location in your home.
2. Show the child the "time-out chair" and tell them this is where they will sit for a short time when they misbehave. Tell the child he or she will sit for the number of minutes that matches their age.
3. You, the parent, will be the only one who decides the child will "go to time-out."
4. Tell the child there will be no distractions during the time-out: no conversation, TV playing, toys in the vicinity of the time-out chair, or

taunting siblings. They must sit quietly for the time-out to begin, and it will end in a short time.

5. Have the child sit in the chair for the first time.
6. Tell the child that you will always be close by while they are in time-out. Some children will need their parent to sit across from them the first few times you use the time-out chair.
7. Consider your child's age. If she is two, make the time-out for two minutes. If he is three, three minutes; if five, five minutes.
8. You will tell them when the time-out is over or (if you prefer) you can use an egg timer with a bell that sounds when the time is up.
9. If the child cries, argues, yells, begs, or leaves the chair before the time-out is over, the time-out will start again; and will not begin until the child sits quietly in the time-out chair.
10. If the child runs out of the chair, gently but firmly place them back in the chair and start the time-out again.
11. When the time-out is over, bend down and talk to the child at eye level. Have them look directly at you. Ask them in a calm voice, "What did you do that got you into time-out?" After a time or two of this question being asked while in time-out, kids learn quickly that they need to arrive at a truthful answer.

Here is an example of a parent using the time-out procedure with his five-year-old:

Molly was eating a dish of ice cream at the kitchen table that her daddy had given her. Her six-year-old sister Megan was sitting across from her, also eating a bowl of ice cream. Molly was sure that Megan had gotten two scoops of ice cream, and she had gotten one. The more Molly watched her sister enjoying her ice cream, the madder she felt inside at this ice cream injustice. When Daddy's back was turned, Molly kicked Megan under the kitchen table. Megan immediately dropped her spoon and howled.

"Ahhhh! Daddy, Molly kicked me."

"Did not!"

"Did too! Daddy . . . !"

"Molly Ann, did you kick Megan?"

"It was an accident."

"No it wasn't. . . . I'm gonna kick you back!"

"No, Megan, you're not." Daddy said and picked up Molly's ice cream dish and put it in the freezer. "Molly, go to the time-out chair."

"Daddy, it's not fair; Megan got more than I did."

"Megan got the same amount of ice cream. Molly, go to the time-out chair."

Molly reluctantly got up from the table and walked to the laundry room where the time-out chair was located. Daddy set the egg timer for five minutes. "I'll be back when the bell rings, Molly." Molly sat quietly in the chair and waited for the bell to ring. Molly thought about what she did. She decided that she should not have kicked Megan, but she deserved more ice cream.

Daddy returned when the egg timer bell rang. Daddy bent down next to Megan's chair.

"Your time-out is over. Look at me, Molly. What did you do to get into time-out?"

"I wanted more ice cream. I kicked Megan."

"You didn't go into time-out because you wanted more ice cream."

"No . . . ., it's cause I kicked Megan. Cause I got mad inside."

"That's right. What is the rule about hitting?"

"Never hit nobody."

"That's right. And what is the reminder?"

"You hit, you sit."

"And that is why you went to time-out?"

"Yes. I'm sorry. I tell Megan I'm sorry, too."

"Please do that. Now let's go back and finish your ice cream."

Simple, quick, and over; that is the essence of the successful time-out.

What Else to Know about Time-Out

Escort or direct your child to the time-out chair *immediately* after the misbehavior. This is not a time for discussion or recriminations; just tell the child in a calm, clear, matter-of-fact manner "Go to the time-out chair." If the child senses that you're uncertain that they must go to time-out, it will almost certainly invite an argument or an emotional meltdown.

In an instance of misbehavior where more than one child is involved, extend the time-out to include all actors. You may need to be a little creative—one child is in the time-out chair while the other sits on the couch—but do not let children make the decision for you about who deserves a time-out.

If you are out of the house and need to use time-out, think ahead about where you will be and what you can do. If you are at the store and the child needs a time-out, take them back out to the car and while you sit in the front seat have them sit quietly in the back seat. If you are attending religious services, at the park, or in someone's office or home, look for a suitable spot for your child to sit quietly for a few minutes, or return to the car.

Time-out is designed to give the child an opportunity to slow down, relax, and think about what just happened. Because of this some kids who have had experience with time-out will sometimes say, "I need a time-out!" When they do, let them have it. When my daughter was young enough for time-out, my wife and I called her giving herself a time-out "Kaitlyn Time."

It is also perfectly okay for adults to give *themselves* a time-out. This is widely prescribed in anger management training. Give yourself a five-minute mental vacation rather than say or do something that you'll regret—especially with your kids; further, what a wonderful way to model and teach self-control to your children.

Emotional Meltdowns

Is there ever a time when it is advisable to *not* have a child take a time-out? Yes, when a child is having an emotional meltdown and escalates into being a danger to themselves or others. The child may whine and complain and argue about the injustice of it all, but when the child continues on with a screaming, crying, kicking, fist-and-object throwing fit, a time-out will not do. Instead, *restrain* the child. There is a *right* way and there is certainly a *wrong* way to restrain a child. Restraint means to calmly and nonviolently intervene in the child's emotional meltdown.

This is what you do: When the child is out of control and using physical means to destroy and cause harm, come from *behind* the child and gently wrap your arms around them and then sit with them. Take any objects they are using to cause harm out of their hands. Tell the child in a low, calm, even voice: "Calm down. When you calm down I will let you go. Calm down and I will let you go. Calm down." Do not say anything else. Most children will relax quickly—although some kids may struggle for a minute longer. When the child is calm, let them go and have them sit in a chair. Give them a moment to compose themselves. At that point you can talk to them as you would if they were finished with a time-out. With children with a repeated history of meltdowns, you will likely need to repeat this nonviolent procedure until they can manage themselves. But you are also training the child to manage their emotions, not just now but also in the future. The child will learn quickly that emotional meltdowns will not produce the results that they want, but being calm just might.

Emotional Meltdown Prevention

If you use this procedure and you do not see an immediate reversal in emotional meltdowns do not be discouraged; it will usually take some repeated trials. What you can do to help prevent meltdowns altogether is watch for signs that your child is becoming emotionally agitated to the degree that they are approaching the point of a meltdown (crying, angry words and gestures). When you see this behavior move down to the child's eye level and say in a low, calm, even voice: "Look at me. I see you are upset. Sit down and I will talk with you." Sitting down is a signal to the body to relax. "Sit down and I'll talk with you." Your intent is to hear the child's perspective of what is causing the child to be on the verge of a meltdown and to help them avert it. Use the listening and paraphrasing skills that are explained in the next chapter. These skills can help avert and stop emotional meltdowns and will help teach your child to practice self-control and self-discipline.

SHAPING

Shaping is a very common psychological technique to establish a new behavior. Shaping involves using positive reinforcement in small bits to reward small bits of the behavior that you wish to see. To use a crude example, if you wish to teach your dog to fetch a ball you reward the dog with a small treat, a pat on the head, or verbal praise, when he first chases the ball, then brings it back to you, lets the ball go, and so forth. In each step of the ball-fetching process, the animal learns quickly that a little more is required to earn the reward. Eventually, he fetches the ball without any positive reinforcement because the behavior is established. Now, your child is not a dog, but the shaping principle is the same. Shaping involves rewarding small bits of positive behavior with positive rewards. Eventually, the rewards are faded out and the positive behavior remains.

Pinpointing and Targeting the Desired Behavior

To start, you want to *pinpoint* and then *target* the behavior that you want to see changed.

Pinpointing means that we describe in behavioral terms exactly what we want to see happen. If we say "I want her to follow directions" or "I want him to get along with other kids" we haven't said exactly what it is we want the child to *do* or *not do*. "I want her to not run away from us when we are in the store," or "I want him to stop hurting other kids," is pinpointing the behavior change that we seek.

Once we have pinpointed the behavior change, we can target the desired behavior. We have a consequence rule for the young child of, "When in the store, always stay where mom or dad can see you" or "Never wrestle anyone to the ground or take anything that does not belong to you." These target behaviors are now ones that we are going to specifically target for elimination. Let's look at two examples: Amy and Julio.

Four-year-old Amy is in the habit of running off from her parent's presence when they shop in stores. When the parent's attention is diverted Amy runs down the store aisle and sometimes around the corner and out of sight. The parents pinpoint the behavior: they want Amy to stay within eyesight the entire time they are shopping and in the store. They target the behavior: Amy will follow the eyesight rule every time they are in a store.

Five-year-old Julio is in the habit of playing very rough with other children. He will wrestle them to the ground and then take their toys or other things he wants. The parents pinpoint the behavior: They want Julio to never wrestle children to the ground or take anything that does not belong to him. They target the behavior: Julio will follow the wrestling and not taking things from others rule.

Shaping the Desired Behavior

And once you have pinpointed the behavior, you can begin actively using shaping to change it. Here's how Amy's and Julio's parents used shaping to get the results that they wanted.

Amy and the department store: Amy's parents told her that they were going to work together on changing her running off behavior in stores. They took Amy to a large department store. When they arrived they reminded Amy of the staying within eyesight of her parents rule while in the store. The parents assured Amy that they knew she could be a "big girl" and follow the rule.

At first, they brought Amy into the store and "practiced" getting a shopping cart and walking around the entrance for about two minutes. After two minutes, they walked back toward the car and immediately praised Amy for walking with them for the entire time. They then walked back into the store entrance, got a shopping cart, and added walking up and down the first three aisles. They walked back to the parking lot and while Amy was praised she was given a piece of sugarless candy. The next day the family returned to the department store, repeated the process, and added more aisles to walk down. Amy ran down the aisle once and her parents took her out to the car for a time-out. The parents told Amy that if she could continue the desired behavior for three days there would be a special outing at the park. Everyone had a good time at the park.

The next week, when the parents needed to shop at the store, they praised Amy every time that she followed the rule about staying within eyesight of her parents. Thereafter, the parents praised Amy periodically for her "good" behavior in the store and she no longer needed reminders.

Julio and the playground: Julio's parents had a more difficult time shaping his behavior, but they didn't give up. The parents explained to Julio their concern about his aggressiveness when playing with other children, and what the consequence rule was for wrestling others to the ground and taking their things. The family lived in a large apartment complex with many young children.

The complex provided a small playground for the children. Julio was told that because of his behavior history, one of his parents would go out with him to the playground three times a day for fifteen minutes each time and watch his behavior. The first day Julio disobeyed the rule and wrestled a child to the ground and took his rubber ball. The parent immediately removed Julio from the playground, had Julio return the ball with an "I'm sorry," and escorted him back into the apartment for a five-minute time-out. That afternoon Julio tried again. He did better but still put his hands on children. The third session Julio did fine. The parents praised Julio for his success the third time. After two weeks of up-and-down behavior, Julio began to be consistently success-ful in following the rule. His parents praised Julio and increased his play-ground time to 20 minutes, then 30 minutes, and then Julio could play at the playground until his schedule required that he do something else. After sev-eral months, Julio rarely, if ever, wrestled children to the ground or took their things.

PUNISHMENTS THAT YOU SHOULD NEVER USE

Some punishments are harsh, cruel, and immoral. Some are also illegal. Needless to say, we should never use them with our children; but some parents do use them—whether they have the desired effect they wanted or not. I've engaged in therapy with parents who forced their young children to take cold showers, locked them in dark rooms, made them stand for hours, made them run for miles, or forced them to dig trenches. Some parents slap their child's face or buttocks with force, pull their hair, kick them, punch them, beat them, and torture them. Also parents who consistently humiliate their children, scream at them, call them wretched names, give them the silent treatment for days, socially isolate them, and deliberately threaten and frighten them.

Some of these parents are mentally ill. Some are sadists who enjoy inflict-ing pain. Some are parents who in a moment of madness give in to the worst impulses against the most defenseless and innocent. Refuse to be one of these parents.

Table 6.1 lists some general categories of punishments you should avoid. If you, or someone you love, have a history of using any of these punish-ments with your children, seek therapy, and commit yourself to learning to use the discipline skills in this book. The goal of discipline is to change unwanted, negative behavior by teaching and providing the opportunity to learn to choose wanted positive behavior. Punishments such as these only teach the child to try and avoid the punishment in the future. They also teach the child to fear and to hate and to live in hopelessness, which is no way to live at all.

Table 6.1.   Punishments You Should Never Use

Physical pain or distress

Restraint
(except briefly if the child is in danger of hurting himself or others)

Extended social isolation

Humiliation

Chapter Seven

Communication That Gets the Results You Want

Good communication requires, more than anything else, having good communication *skills*. This chapter will help you acquire those skills. Take your time to master each of the eight communication skills. Wait until you have mastered one through practice before adding another. To try to learn and use all the skills at once will be burdensome and confusing, and make you sound like a robot. The skills are:

- The five B's of communication
- Social conversation
- Giving feedback
- Straight talk
- Taking notice
- Paraphrasing
- The "I" statement
- Asking for what you want

THE FIVE B'S OF COMMUNICATION

The first set of skills is basic and essential to all communication with your child. I call it "the five B's of communication": Be specific, be clear, be behavioral, be brief, and be open. We'll look at what is involved in each one.

Be Specific

Stick to one issue at a time. You want to talk to your child about how he felt when his absent parent didn't call on his birthday. Avoid mixing in your personal feelings about the absent parent (what a louse he is, and how this is an example of how undependable he was when you were married, etc.). With unrelated issues, your message becomes confused and is lost. Better to focus on just the one issue, that is, your child's feelings about his parent not calling.

> *Not Specific*: "Tim, too bad your dad didn't call. Want cake?"
> *Specific*: "Tim, I'd like to talk to you about your dad not calling on your birthday."

Be Clear

Learn to choose and weigh your words carefully. Cliché though it is, "Think before you speak" is nonetheless good advice. Choose words that convey acceptance and understanding. Avoid words that are heavily laden with emotions and tend to provoke anger or upset. Say what you mean in simple, plain language. You need not be profound, hysterical, or theatrical to get your message across.

> *Unclear:* "You'll have to pay all of your expenses."
> *Clear:* "Now that you have a new bicycle, you'll need to pay all of your expenses from your allowance for a lock, headlight, and tag."

Be Behavioral

Talk about behavior, not attitudes. Behavior, or its effects, can be seen; attitudes cannot. It doesn't do any good to tell your child, "Improve your attitude toward your schoolwork." What is it that you want your child to *do* or *not do*? If you want a change in behavior or wish to comment on behavior, you need to say what *action* you want or what effects you have seen.

> *Not behavioral:* "I want to thank you for all of your hard work today."
> *Behavioral:* "I want to thank you for cutting the grass and raking the leaves. It was hard work and you did a super job."

Be Brief

Get to the point quickly. Most children will tune you out when you sermonize, harangue, or shout. It is useless to say the same thing over again and again, only louder. Speak calmly and concisely. If you are too emotional, your child typically will not hear your words, only the anger, disappointment, sorrow, or other emotion. He will react emotionally to the emotions you convey, which does nothing to facilitate communication.

Not Brief: "I'm disappointed and sad that you quit Little League. But I understand that it was your choice. I just wish young people today would learn to stick it out when the coach doesn't play you right away. That's when things get tough, and the tough get going. Now, when I was your age . . ."

Brief: "I'm disappointed and sad that you decided to quit Little League."

Be Open

Convey the opportunity for your child to speak *and your willingness to listen.* Your child wants more than anything else to have someone listen and acknowledge her feelings. Acknowledgment is not the same as agreement. You may not agree with or be able to accept your child's message. Often that is not what your child is seeking; she does want someone to listen. With an open heart, ask her to tell you what she is thinking and feeling, and then listen with an open mind.

Not Open: "I can't believe you'd say that. Now, you don't really believe that, and you don't have any reason to think that way."

Open: "What I hear you saying is that you believe I am unfair and unreasonable."

With practice, you can master these five basic communication skills. Some parents make a deliberate attempt to practice the skills on a daily basis until they feel they are using them consistently. Other parents ask the child to help them practice the skills: during a five-minute conversation, the child is asked to take particular note of the things her parent says, and to note if they were specific, clear, behavioral, brief, and open.

As parents practice these communication skills and others in this chapter, they often report that their kids start to imitate them. This is all to the good. Kids will imitate each other as well. The communication skills you teach your child by example will serve him well in his relationships with other people and over the course of their entire life. People cherish other people who are skilled communicators. As parents, being admired and respected for our excellent communication skills will help us in every other aspect of parenting.

SOCIAL CONVERSATION

Having simple social conversation with your child on a regular basis will pay handsomely not only in improving your communication skills as a parent, but also in strengthening the parent-child relationship. Good communication is the heart and soul of rapport.

Good conversation is more than just taking turns talking. Unfortunately, research shows that in the average American home, most "talk time" between children and their parents is concerned with making requests and demands. Kids ask their parents for things or services, and parents make demands for things or services. Often the total talk time per week is reduced to a few minutes in the morning and again in the evening. When all parents hear are phrases like "Mom, I need a clean shirt!" and all the child hears is "If you need a clean shirt, you'll need to wash it yourself—I don't have time" there is little basis for building a relationship.

Listen more than you talk. A Greek philosopher once said: "We have two ears but only one mouth that we may hear more and speak less"—still good advice.

You can shoot the breeze while preparing dinner or during mealtime, while you're riding together in the car, while forsaking fifteen minutes of the evening news show. It doesn't really matter what the topic is—their day, your day, an incident that involved someone else, school, work, local, national, or world events; or even the weather—basically anything that you would talk with an adult about in the same fashion is appropriate.

Children, like almost everyone else, prefer to talk about themselves or things that interest them, which may not interest you. If you get past this obstacle, let your child know that you admire and respect him, or acknowledge some thought, talent, skill, or action he has taken. Talk in a friendly and positive manner. Finally, impose a one-minute gag rule on yourself. After speaking for one minute, stop and offer your child a chance to talk.

Open and Closed Questions

A useful tool to engage children in conversation is to ask open questions. An open question is one that cannot be answered with a simple yes or no.

"What did you do in school today?"

"What big plans do you have for the weekend?"

"What did you enjoy the most playing at the park today?"

You may still get a shrug or a one-word response, but by asking open questions you are much more likely to get a detailed response that could lead to a pleasant and interesting conversation with your child. People tend to like and appreciate people whom they know. Asking open questions in a friendly tone will help you get to know and have a likable relationship with your child.

A closed question is just the opposite of an open question. You can answer it with a one-word reply. How was school today? Fine. Learning anything interesting? No. Got any homework? Yes. You want chicken or hamburger for dinner? Chicken. Do you have your soccer practice on Saturday? Yes. Anything new with your friends? No. Okay, anything you want to talk about? No. See? I try to talk to the kid and he never says anything!

Of course, there is nothing wrong with closed questions—sometimes you need to ask them. To stimulate conversation, however, you need to vary closed questions with open ones.

Listening Cues

When you do engage your child in conversation, you want to let her know you are listening by using effective listening cues. Here is what you do:

- Maintain eye contact.
- Nod and smile occasionally.
- When sitting, lean forward slightly.
- Use an occasional encourager: "Uh huh." "Interesting." "Really?" "Is that so?"

Using these listening cues tells your child you are engaged in what she is saying, and you want to hear more. These cues open the door to quality communication.

GIVING FEEDBACK

At some point in your conversation with your child, you may want to offer feedback. Feedback simply means your turn to talk about what you think. Effective feedback is not critical; it is honest and straightforward. You get to offer feedback for being such a good listener.

There is no hard-and-fast rule about what you should say in giving feedback. You may want to offer advice, if it's asked for, or your own opinions or observations. You may offer possible solutions to problems or sympathy, if they are warranted. You may offer nothing more than acknowledgment, and paraphrase and summarize what you have heard. Sometimes the most effective feedback is not to make any comment at all, but only to listen, especially if the child is angry.

Further, not all feedback is verbal. A caring touch, hug, or kiss can say more than the most eloquent words. Likewise, sometimes a child's behavior says a great deal more than her words, and you can comment on that.

To describe the behavior you see, use feedback words like withdrawn, fearful, anxious, upset, confused, hurt, worried, or angry; happy, excited, energetic, silly, pleased, or proud.

- You seem to be upset. Do you want to talk?
- Can I help you? You seem to be confused.

- You sure are happy today.
- You seem really excited.
- You look like you're lost in thought.

Most kids appreciate your noticing and being sensitive to their moods. Your feedback can also help them be aware of what they are thinking and feeling, which can lead to an interesting conversation with you.

On the other hand, when children will not talk to their parents, it's often not that they *can't* talk to their parents, it's that they are *fearful* of talking to them. Some kids are fearful of stinging criticism, the lash of the parent's anger, or the perception that when they do talk, they are misunderstood. Some kids simply do not have ready access to their feelings or the words to articulate how they feel or what they want to say.

Most parents want to believe that they have made the opportunity to talk to them easy for their children. To do this, you want to leave the door of opportunity wide open for them to come to you with their problems and concerns, failures and triumphs, hopes and plans, and to express their everyday needs, too. You want your child to have the certain knowledge that you will always have a receptive ear and a compassionate heart. When children receive consistently positive and useful feedback from their parents they will believe that they are being heard.

Here are some especially useful things to know about offering feedback to your child:

- Be clear about the purpose of the feedback: "I wanted to comment on your plans for the party."
- Describe the specific behavior for which you are providing feedback: "I noticed that you didn't invite your brother to the party."
- Describe the consequences of her behavior: "I think he'll be hurt that you didn't invite him."
- Ask for your child's response: "What do you think?"
- If a behavior change is sought, discuss the alternatives: "You can make a point of asking him yourself."
- Summarize and express your confidence and support: "So you'll talk to your brother as soon as he comes home from practice and invite him to the party. I think that is a great idea and he'll be pleased."

STRAIGHT TALK

Someone once said the art of raising children is stepping on their toes without messing up the shine on their shoes. In the same vein, the art of offering advice or criticism to children is to convey it in a way that lets the child keep the shine on his shoes while he feels pressure on his feet. Using the skill of straight talk will do this nicely.

Straight talk means that you say exactly what you think in behavioral terms. You say it straight, without hesitation or reserve, using the five B's of communication; and you leave out accusing or demeaning language. Here is an example of parent and child using straight talk.

"Randy, I want to talk to you about your friends, and I want to use straight talk."

"Go ahead."

"My straight talk is that you've been very rude to several of your friends."

"When was this?"

"When you've had your friends over to watch the game the last several times. I've heard you call them some very nasty names."

"They know I'm just kidding."

"They may be hurt by it and may not want to say anything."

"They call me names, too. It's just fooling around."

"They may not want to say anything for fear of hurting your friendship. I think it is very rude and disrespectful and I would like you to stop doing it."

"Straight talk?"

"Go ahead."

"I think you are making too much of it. I don't mean it in a mean way. If my friends were hurt by it, they would tell me to knock it off. We know that we can say stuff like that to each other because we are friends."

"I would like you to stop doing it when you are around me."

"I can do that, Dad."

Now, how do you get your kids in the habit of hearing your straight talk? First, as a parent did in the example, you *preface* your message by saying "straight talk?" This signals that what you're about to say is going to be frank and forthright. Second, you get the other person's *consent* to use straight talk. This way the person on the receiving end of the straight talk cannot deny that you have permission to speak freely and openly. Third, in order to *use* straight talk you must be willing to *hear* straight talk. Straight talk implies that you are willing to give as well as to receive information and engage in dialogue.

After using straight talk a few times your child may say "No, I'd rather not hear straight talk just now." That's okay. Remember, straight talk is designed to give advice or constructive criticism, not directives necessarily. It is a very handy communication tool that is respectful while at the same time being honest and straightforward. Like stepping on toes while maintaining shines.

TAKING NOTICE

The only time some kids get feedback from their parents is when they do something wrong. In fact, the only way these kids know that their behavior has been pleasing to their parents is when they haven't been yelled at lately. This is not as it should be.

Take notice of specific behaviors that you like and want to see repeated. Praise your child for this behavior as close in time as possible to when you first took notice of its occurrence.

Close in Time

"Hey, when I came in I saw you washed the car. That's great."

"You're home right on time. Excellent."

"I see you prepared a wonderful lunch for us. Thank you."

Use feeling words such as "like," "appreciate," glad," and "happy." Leave out "stinger" words or phrases: "I'm so glad to see you doing that—*and it's about time you did*"; "I sure appreciate your *finally* being more responsible."

Role Model

Children take more frequent notice of what we *do* than what we *say*. Model the behavior you like and want to see your child repeat: speak courteously, help others, obey laws, complete chores and tasks, read books, listen attentively, attend religious services, and the like.

Spread the Word

Tell others what your child has done or is doing that you like. Lean over the fence and tell the neighbor what a great job he did trimming the shrubs. Talk about your child's success at family gatherings. Tell the teacher how proud you are of your daughter's homework and behavior in class. Word of your praise will get back to your kids. And, of course, praise them directly such as at the dinner table when they can't help but hear. The easiest way to remember to offer praise is to take notice of the behavior you like and want to see repeated and comment on it.

PARAPHRASING

Once you engage in active communication with your child, you'll want to use an occasional paraphrase. Paraphrasing is a powerful communication tool.

To paraphrase, you use your own words to restate what you've heard your child say to you. As you gain experience using paraphrasing, you'll be able to reflect not only your child's words, but also the underlying feelings. This often helps your child clarify what he is thinking and feeling by having someone else listen and reflect what he said.

Helpful phrases to begin a paraphrase include:

- "Sounds like . . ." "What I hear you saying is . . ." "Tell me if I understand . . ."
- "Sounds like you are confused about what to do next."
- "What I hear you saying is that you have three different choices and you are struggling a bit about which one to choose."
- "Tell me if I understand. Dave and Jeremy have chosen to do this, and you want to be supportive of your friends, but you don't feel that, all things considered, this is the right choice for you."

Alternatively, you can comment on know what you think the underlying feeling is that has been described:

- "You were hurt and surprised when that happened."
- "I'll bet that was exciting!"
- "It must have been great to see Rick again."

If you have it wrong, don't worry—kids will tell you. Most kids appreciate your using an occasional paraphrase. It tells them you are actively listening and at least trying to understand what they are attempting to communicate to you.

The parents kids admire the most are the ones who they say "really listen" and "understand" their feelings and concerns. By using the skill of paraphrasing you'll earn just such a reputation with your child. This will pay huge dividends in your having a quality relationship with your child.

Echo Technique

Paraphrasing is a very useful tool but one that some parents find difficult to get the hang of with ease. While you are practicing, you might use a similar but easier tool called the echo technique. Simply repeat the last few words the child said. Here is an example.

"I don't feel like I can trust Vinnie anymore. He's lied to me too often. He says he doesn't have any interest in Robin, they're just friends, but I've seen them walking together in the hallways and they look very cozy to me."

"Very cozy, okay."

"Yeah, and I know they like text message each other all day."

"All day."

"Yes, so I'm thinking about talking to both of them. But I don't know if I'll do it separately or together. I just want to know where I stand."

"Where you stand."

You don't need to echo every phrase, but this communication technique is a good way to indicate to your child that you are actively listening and understanding.

THE "I" STATEMENT

Another useful communication tool is the "I" statement." The "I" statement has three interrelated parts:

- A behavior description
- Your feelings about the behavior
- Your want or need for behavior change

Here are two examples.

"Chris, when you are not dressed and ready to go in the morning, I feel very annoyed. I want you to be dressed and ready to eat breakfast by 6:30 am."

"Chris, I really appreciate your being dressed and ready to eat breakfast by 6:30 every morning this week. That's super. Now I need you to have all of your school supplies in your backpack and ready to go when we leave the house."

In an "I" statement you can say "I want . . . ," "I need . . . ," "I expect. . . ." You're taking responsibility for your feelings when you do. You're telling the child (or spouse, relative, neighbor, friend, coworker) what you perceive is happening and you are *requesting* a specific behavior change.

Often, being made aware of how your behavior is affecting someone else is enough to motivate change, but not always. An "I" statement implies a choice, rather than being a directive. Telling your child you would like something to happen means there is still the option of doing it or not doing it. There is nothing wrong with stating a request or desire, but an "I" statement will not mandate that your child (or anyone else) comply with your desires. If Chris doesn't give a rat's rear about his mother's annoyance with him wasting time in the morning, the "I" statement will fall on deaf ears.

The "I" statement usually works best with sensitive children who are sensitive to their parent's and other people's feelings and are considerate of other people's wishes. All they may need is to know what you want. "I" statements can be very effective communication tools with kids like this.

Here is a sample script to use for the "I" statement: "When you . . . I feel . . . I would like/I need/I expect . . . Thank you."

By using "I" statements, you can also model for children how to ask for the things that they want. Kids (and parents) often *think* they are asking when they whine, complain, pout, threaten, cajole, cry, beg, guilt trip, or get angry. Through "I" statements they can learn how to state exactly how they feel about a situation directly to the person or people involved and ask them to make a change. They are often amazed at getting what they want—and so are their parents.

ASKING FOR WHAT YOU WANT

Communication quickly breaks down between parents and their kids when parents fail to ask for what they want. Unfortunately, some parents fail routinely, and by their example, teach their children to do the same.

Sometimes when parents want a child to do something or understand something, they use a shorthand version of mental telepathy that involves using their child's name coupled with an unclear demand: "Brad, knock it off!" "Oh, Ape-rull, stop doing that!" or, when they are especially exacerbated, they use all three names—"Juan Luis Ramirez, don't bug me!" Unless your child is quite adept at mind reading, this usually does little good. What exactly is it that you want the child to do or not do? How will he (and you) know that he is doing it?

There is a better way.

MINIMAL EFFECTIVE RESPONSE

Start with an "I" statement. If your "I" message is ignored or disregarded by your child, you may need to escalate your response. You can learn how to calmly and assertively ask for what you want by using a technique that psychologists David Rimm and John Masters called the "minimal effective response." The idea is to use the minimal degree of effort to promote behavior change in someone else. To use this technique, say what you want in behavioral terms. If the message is disregarded, you can calmly but assertively escalate the message until you get what you want. Here are a number of different ways a parent can respond to the same situation.

Unclear demand: "I'm studying, tone down the racket!"

Overkill: "I can't study! If you don't shut the hell up, you can't have your friends at the house for a month!"

Underkill: "Honey, please. I'm studying for an exam and I sure would appreciate it if you could keep the noise down just a teensy-weensy bit. Sorry to interrupt. Thank you. I love you."

The minimal effective response is a better alternative, escalating through the three statements as needed. Lead off with an "I" statement.

"When you and your friends make so much noise, I can't study for my exam. I want you and them to be quieter while I'm studying. Thank you."

If this does not have the desired effect, use the minimal effective response.

- "Look, I've asked you to please be more quiet. I simply cannot concentrate on my studying while the TV is so loud and your friends are talking."
- "Turn down the TV and speak more softly while I'm studying for my exam."
- "Turn off the TV and go outside with your friends to talk."

When you ask for what you want in a firm and calm manner, you will usually get what you want—and avoid conflict—on the first try. However, by using the minimal effective response when the "I" message has failed to convey what you want, you can then escalate the message until the behavior change you want comes about. If you wind up getting into an argument use the argument deflectors or the script technique to get your point across.

Script Technique

You can write a script for what you want to say and then repeat the script for different situations: a coming-home-after-curfew script, a fighting-with-your-brother script, a do-your chores/homework-now script, and so on. You can write out your script and read it aloud or say it from memory when the time comes. Scripts are not sermonettes. Say what you want to say in the form of an "I" statement or demand, simply, clearly, and quickly. Using this tool may seem a bit ludicrous at first, but it's better than becoming angry or overly emotional when you want to get your point across to your child and you can't find the words.

The five B's of communication, plus open questions, listening cues, feedback, straight talk, social conversation, paraphrasing, the echo technique, "I" statements, the minimal effective response, and the script technique are all communication tools that stimulate, encourage, and promote parent-child communication. If you make the time and take the effort to practice using them, you will enjoy a quality relationship with your child.

COMMUNICATION BLOCKS

Just as there are communication habits that encourage and stimulate conversation with children, there are two habits that block communication: parent deafness and coercion cycles.

Parent Deafness

Parents can literally train a child to ignore them. A child who is parent deaf is deaf to parental demands. It is not that he doesn't hear—he hears fine—it is that he has been trained not to respond. The child knows from experience that when Mom or Dad says that something needs to happen, it doesn't. Mom and Dad don't mean what they say and say what they mean. The demand can be safely ignored.

Most parentally deaf children start losing their hearing when they are very young. The deafness then accelerates when they become adolescents. The three-year-old is told not to do some obnoxious behavior . . . and told, and warned, and threatened, and told again. Finally, the parent gives up and the child does as he pleases.

As the child gets older, she learns from experience she doesn't really have to come to the dinner table on the first call, she doesn't really have to be in by a set time, and she doesn't really have to do the chore if she doesn't feel like doing it. She also learns she doesn't need to respond until her parent calls her to the dinner table for the fifth time, nothing will happen as a result of staying out three hours past the set time, and her parents will do the chore because it is easier that way. As they become older, the child learns to extrapolate from these experiences and discovers it is "okay" to talk back to her parents, that she can skip school, smoke dope, and date any boy she wants, because her parents no longer bother to put a stop to it. Mom and Dad do not say what needs to be said, and do not do what needs to be done. The result is children who are deaf to their parent's demands.

How do you get your kids to hear you? The cure for parent deafness is consistency, clarity, and follow-through.

Consistency means consistently giving the same message every time. If your child must comply this time but not the next, the resulting inconsistency on your part breeds disbelief in, and contempt for, your parental word.

Clarity means being clear. Telling your child to "knock it off," "stop it, I said," and "quit doing that or you'll be sorry" tells them nothing. Specify the behavior that you want to see altered in the demand.

Follow-through means imposing consequences immediately. Nothing gets our attention like results. Nothing underlines our message like follow through. When children learn that they are consistently choosing a negative consequence that goes with the negative behavior, they then alter their behavior in their own best interest.

Coercion Cycles

Sometimes parents and kids find themselves circling around the same issue again and again. This is usually because parent and child are in a cycle of failed communication. The parent never gets her point across to the child, and the child never strives to get the point. Instead, parent and child play a communication game where both wind up feeling angry and alienated from one another. Psychologist Gerald Patterson calls these wacky communication breakdowns *coercion cycles*. The common elements of coercion cycles include: anger and irritation, denial and defensiveness, and placating and appeasement.

Scott: Scott's mother walked into the house carrying a full bag of groceries from the car. She was hot and tired and had decided that supper would be a frozen dinner this evening. As she peered into the living room she could see Scott sprawled out on the couch, watching that damn MTV, with his dirty socks propped up on the armrest. That did it.

"Scott! What are you doing?"

"I'm watching TV."

"You're supposed to be watching your little brother, not TV."

"I am watching him."

"Is he in his room?"

"He's around."

"Where is he exactly? Josh is only four years old. I wish you would be more responsible."

"He's around."

"Go look for him."

"I will as soon as this is over."

"Is he in his room?"

"He's around."

"As long as he's in his room, that's fine."

"He is."

"Okay, then. You want the roast beef or the turkey loaf?"

As Scott's mother began to place the frozen dinners in the microwave oven, Josh came running into the house from the backyard. She told Josh to wash his hands for dinner. Josh ran into the living room and began to ride his tricycle in circles. Scott was watching a video of a young woman with blue hair and wearing a spiked dog collar, who was screaming into a microphone about wanting freedom from oppression. It was only after dinner that mother discovered that Josh had decided to repaint the outside walls with a red permanent marker.

Kelly: Kelly was excited. She was sure that she would be getting her running shoes—the ones with the little red lights in the soles. Kelly's father examined the shoes when Kelly handed them to him with a pleading look on her face. The shoes looked fine—until dad saw the $200 price tag hanging from the shoelaces.

"What? $200! I don't think so, Kelly."

"Dad," Kelly explained patiently, "these are special, I need them."

"Need them for what? You're not a track star."

"I need them for school."

"Why does a seventh grader need $200 running shoes to wear to school?"

"Dad, you want me to look like a dork? Everyone is wearing these."

"Why is everyone wearing these?"

"Because they're cool, that's why," Kelly said with rising exasperation.

"Kelly, we can't afford these shoes."

"But I need them."

"What is the matter with these shoes over here?" Dad asked in a reasonable tone as he moved over to a counter with $50 sneakers. "You can have one of these."

"Why?" Kelly asked. "Why do you always make me take the lousy stuff?"

"Kelly, I don't . . ."

"Yes, you do!" Kelly started to cry. "I never get anything!"

"Honey, $200 is half of our school clothes budget."

"Dadd-dee! Pleazzzzzzzze! I need them."

"Oh, Kelly. Please don't make a scene. Let's have lunch, then come back and finish our shopping, okay?"

Kelly began to wail.

"Kelly . . ."

Kelly began to stagger around the aisle under the weight of her grief. People were looking.

"Kelly . . . Okay, okay, okay, if it means that much to you. Let's get the damn shoes."

Kelly's tears started to subside. She began to feel better. Now she could look cool—especially at night when everyone can see the little red lights in the soles of her ultra-cool $200 shoes. As they walked up to the register, and Dad took out his credit card, he realized that he felt exhausted and broke. But hey, at least Kelly was happy, and he would not let this happen again when they got to the jeans department.

Coercion Cycles Stopped

The antidote to coercion cycles is the five B's of communication. That is framing your communication to your child in words that are specific, clear, behavioral, brief, and open. Let's replay these scenes.

Scott:

"Scott! Are you watching your little brother?"

"Yeah, I'm watching him."

"Where is he right now?"

"He's in his room."

"Do you know that for certain?"

"Yeah, he's in there."

"I want you to get up off the couch, go look for him, and come and tell me where he is and what he has been up to."

"I will as soon as this is over."

"No, Scott. Now. Please do it right now."

Mother stood in the doorway of the living room with an icy stare until Scott, with a heavy sigh and rolling eyes, got up off the couch and went to look for Josh.

"Thank you for your cooperation," Mother said. "Do you want the roast beef or turkey loaf?"

"Turkey loaf," Scott said, as he came through the kitchen on his way to the backyard. A minute later Josh came running into the kitchen from outside. His mother told him to go into the bathroom to wash his hands. Josh raced toward the living room. His mother followed him. Scott walked in behind Josh.

"He was in the yard, with markers in his hand," he said.

"Josh, go to the bathroom and wash your hands with the bar of soap. Get all of the dirt off your hands, rinse them, and then dry them with a towel. Then come in and sit at the kitchen table."

Josh ran toward his tricycle.

"Josh, do it now. If you need help, Scott will help you do it."

Josh climbed carefully off his tricycle and walked slowly to the bathroom. Josh and Scott looked at each other. What was going on? On the way, Josh and Scott heard their mother say, "As soon as dinner is over, Scott, you clear the table and stack the dishes in the dishwasher, and Josh, you go out to the backyard and bring me all of your permanent markers."

Both boys rolled their eyes. It was that stupid parenting class.

Kelly:

Kelly's dad howled, "What! I don't think so, Kelly."

"Dad," Kelly explained patiently, "these are special. I need them."

"You need them for school? We are only buying school clothes right now."

"Well . . . yeah. I need them for school. They're cool."

"Yes, I can see that they're cool, and that you really want them. And the reality is that we can't afford to spend this much on one item."

"Why not?"

"Because we can't afford to spend this much on one item."

"But Dad . . . ."

"You can spend $50 on any pair of sneakers that you like."

"But what about these? I don't want to look like a dork."

"Then I suggest you find a pair that you like that are within our price range."

"But Dad . . ."

"I'm going over to the jeans section while you find a pair of sneakers you like. I'll meet you over there."

"Well, can I at least get a pair of designer jeans?"

"Sure can, as long as you can find a pair that is within our price range."

"Holy cow. I'll shop with Mom from now on."

Being clear, calm, and assertive with children will keep you and them out of coercion cycle entanglement.

Chapter Eight

Conflict Resolution with Children

Some conflict in families is inevitable; but continual conflict and angry encounters with your child are not. Consistent use of the skills in this chapter will help you avoid conflict most of the time. Many problems with children are mundane and only require willingness to problem solve and seek solutions that everyone can live with. Like all the other skills in this book, with practice, you *can* do this.

The following skills go a long ways to facilitate conflict resolution and problem solving:

- Solving specific problems
- Intentional listening
- Workable solutions
- Balancing yes and no

SOLVING SPECIFIC PROBLEMS

A useful tool to use when attempting to problem solve an issue is a problem-solving worksheet (provided on the website). The key is that you and your child work together on this, with mutual respect and a willingness to find solutions. To create a problem-solving worksheet, follow these steps:

1. Write a short description of the problem behavior in behavioral terms.
2. Working with your child, write three or four ideas for possible solutions.
3. Each of you mark whether you think each possible solution *will* work, *might* work, *won't* work. Discuss your reasons, taking into account the possible consequences for each choice.

95

4. Continue to discuss, writing down more ideas if needed, until you both agree on a particular solution. If you simply cannot agree, then put off making a decision until another day.
5. Implement the solution you decide on and schedule a time within a week to a month to review how it's going. Make any needed changes.
6. When you and your child become proficient using the worksheet, you can follow these same procedures orally—simply follow the first five steps—and dispense with using the worksheet, if you like.

This is how one family problem solved an ongoing issue:

1. Describe the problem in simple, clear, direct, behavioral terms: There is a problem with the house lights being left on after everyone has left for the day. When the lights are left on, it runs up the electric bill beyond what we can afford and is an unnecessary expense.
2. Brainstorm and write down three or four possible solutions: (a) Assign one person the job of turning off all the lights before leaving the house. (b) Have each person turn off the lights he/she turned on upon leaving the room. (c) Get automatic timers for all the lights. (d) Budget more money for the light bill each month.
3. What will work, might work, won't work: (a) That will work, but it isn't fair for the same person to have to do it all the time. We would need to rotate responsibility. And each person needs to agree to be aware of the lights they turn on, and strive to turn them off. (b) That could work, but it is not working now, so we have the problem. (c) That's too expensive; we are already struggling to pay the light bill. (d) The same problem as with (c).
4. Agree on a solution you think will work. It looks like (a) is the answer. The last person to leave the house each day checks the rooms to be sure that the lights are out. We'll put a reminder note on the front door. Each person in the family will have the task for one week. We all agree to strive to be aware of the lights we turn on, and then turn them off when we leave the room.
5. Begin using the solution. Review and make any needed changes.

Hooray! The electric bill is down 20 percent this month. However, we are still having lights left on in the back bedrooms. Let's post a reminder note by the door in every room and see if that makes a difference. Let's celebrate our success and go weekend camping.

This problem-solving approach is simple, but very effective. It provides everyone in the family an opportunity to be heard and to contribute directly to the family's success.

INTENTIONAL LISTENING

Listening during conflict resolution and active problem solving requires that you listen with two ears as well as a third. Listen for *why* your child thinks as he or she does about the issue. Listening in this way requires an open mind and constant effort. It is hard, but certainly worth your attention. Listen in these three ways:

1. Listen with an uncritical mind: Try not to make up your mind about what is on your child's mind before she says it. Let your child say what she wants to say, no matter how stupid, insignificant, or wrong you may think it is at the time.
2. Listen with acceptance: Be aware of your body language so that you convey respect. A smirking mouth, bored grin, folded arms, heavy sighs, and glaring/rolling eyes will short-circuit your child's desire to communicate. Instead, while maintaining eye contact and nodding occasionally, lean forward slightly, with your arms resting on your knees.
3. Listen with interest: You can demonstrate interest when you paraphrase responses and ask open questions. Asking open questions implies that you will wait for an answer. When you hear a statement or an opinion with which you disagree (even strongly disagree), ask your child to elaborate and to expand on his answer.

If you don't understand his point, use an encouraging phrase such as "I don't think I understand, but please keep going." Another helpful phrase is "Help me see the other side of this if you do not agree with what I've said about it." Using these phrases *alone* will greatly strengthen the chances that your child will *listen to you* and what you have to say about the issue.

Further, in your own mind, seek to separate fact from subjective opinion. "Charlie, you're a slob" is an opinion. "Charlie, you left your dirty clothes on the bathroom floor" is a fact. Kids will frequently argue and not listen to opinions about themselves; it is much harder to argue with a fact.

Listening in these three ways will earn you a reputation with your child as a parent who listens respectfully and accurately. This reputation alone can help solve problems.

WORKABLE SOLUTIONS

There are a number of well-known and commonsense positions you can assume in negotiating or collaborating that could provide a workable solutions to problems with your child. They are all based on mutual respect and a willingness to cooperate. Matthew McKay, Martha Davis, and Patrick Fanning developed part of the list in their book, *Messages*: *The Communications Skills Book.*

- Take turns: "I'll take out the garbage on the even-numbered weeks if you'll take out the garbage on the odd-numbered weeks."
- Split the difference: "You want me to buy you a new makeup kit. I'll pay half if you'll pay the other half."
- Have a trial: "You can try doing your homework in your room for a month. If your grades drop in any subject, it's back to the kitchen table."
- Cut the pie: "I've made up a list of household chores. Everyone can take turns choosing from the list until all the chores are picked."
- You get what you want, I get what I want: "You can have the sleepover at the house as long as you pay the expenses and there is responsible adult supervision."
- Do both: "You can spend Christmas Eve with me, and Christmas Day with your dad."

BALANCING YES AND NO

Ideally, children should hear a balance of yes and no responses from their parents. Kids never say, "You always say yes! You always let me do everything I want to do. It's not fair." They tend to remember the *no* and forget about the *yes*.

It is not the firm no that upsets most children; it is the superior or hostile tone in which the parent states it: "You've got to be kidding!" "Hell no." "Don't even think about asking me that." "I said no and that's the end of it." "In your dreams, fella." "What part of *no* don't you understand?"

It is better to let your *no* be a *no* and not to dress it up with commentary. Just give a simple *no* and a brief explanation, if one is warranted: "No, you can't be out that late on a school night." "No, that is against the rule." "No, that is not acceptable to me." Often, a simple no will do nicely. Sometimes kids ask just to be sure that the answer really is *no*.

Saying *yes* is easy (and usually a lot more fun). However, you can qualify your yes to make it more explicit as to what you are giving consent to. You can use this phrase: "Yes, but here is what needs to happen . . .": "Yes, but here is what needs to happen when you go to the amusement park on Saturday: either I or Maria's mom will need to go with you; we also need to leave the park by the time it gets dark." You can also use the word *and* instead of the word *but*. "Yes, you can go to the movies with Ramon, *and* you need to be home before 10:00 pm." "Yes, I am fine with you finishing your game first *and* you need to empty the trash." Elaborating on the *yes* in this way will help prevent misunderstanding, conflicts, arguments, and hurt feelings later on.

Chapter Nine

Reinforcers for Behaviors You Want to See Repeated

Why can't parents simply depend upon the avoidance of the adverse conse-quence to deter unwanted child behavior? Isn't that enough to get kids to behave better? For most kids it is not, especially if the misbehavior has a number of built-in incentives to choose it.

BECKY

I once worked with a family in which the nine-year-old daughter was being punished a week for every day of school that she got into a fight. The girl was frustrated, the school was frustrated, and the parents were frustrated because their daughter's behavior in this regard had not improved one bit. Everyone was mad at everybody else.

The key to the solution to this daily physical fighting was to ask the family a simple question: How long was Becky punished for right now? Becky replied wearily, "the rest of my life." Her mother said, "No, honey, its only one month." Her father, wanting to be helpful, said, "I thought it was two months."

Just as I thought, no one in the family had the slightest idea. Each day when Becky got home from school, Becky was told by one of her parents that the school had called and reported her in another fight in her classroom or on the playground. If Becky could not induce a peer to fight over some per-ceived—real or imagined—offense, she would threaten a teacher and de-mand to duke it out. The resulting penalty was Becky racked up another week of losing privileges. No TV, phone, text messaging, visits to or from friends, computer surfing, social outings, or recreational activities of any kind. And yet Becky kept fighting. I asked if home grounding was the only behavioral penalty the parents used. Oh no, the parents said. On school days when Becky was dismissed from school for fighting, she was required to accompany one of her parents to work.

Becky the Brawler—as she came to be known—had not the slightest incentive to avoid getting into fights at school. In fact, she had every good reason—from her perspective—to continue to fight: She could leave school, go to her parents' workplace, and be left mostly alone with a degree of freedom and relaxation she couldn't have at school or home. Her father was part owner of a video arcade, and her mother worked as an instructor at a fitness center. On the days that they took Becky to work with them she got to do all the wonderful things that she could never do while she was in school, or later at home. When with her father, she played video games all day; when with her mother, she swam and played basketball and volleyball or she used the exercise equipment. And, when she got bored enough, she would get into fights with other children or adults and her parents would stop what they were doing and paid constant attention to her.

As it was, Becky had no reasonable prospect of digging herself out of an ever-deepening hole of restriction, so why try? (Her lack of education was of little concern as she was going to be a lady wrestler.)

We wiped the slate clean and started again. I set the family up with a simple contract: for every day that Becky attended school, did satisfactory work, and avoided even so much as an argument, she would have free time to do with as she pleased that evening and weekend—including having play time with the parents and visits in after-school hours to the arcade and the gym. For every instance of fighting or unsatisfactory work, her parents would restrict her freedom for that evening or the weekend—with no play time or after-school visits—and with monitored makeup schoolwork. Becky's parents tracked her attendance and behavior with the Daily Class Assignment Report (provided on the website). After Becky got into a fight twice in the next three weeks—testing the system as it were—and her parents followed up, she never got into another fight at school. Eventually she graduated with her class and today she is a young mother with a child of her own to keep from fighting (she never became a lady wrestler).

RECOGNIZING POSITIVE BEHAVIOR

Every child does things that are cooperative, appropriate, and expected—at least some of the time. No one—not even the most defiant child—is a pain in the neck all of the time. We have, up until now, been emphasizing methods to get your child to discontinue negative behavior and to choose positive behavior as an alternative. I want to show you some very effective skills that will greatly increase the chances of your child choosing not only to *not* do the *wrong* thing, but to *do* the *right* thing.

You and I would not work at our jobs unless we are paid a salary. We also want our medical benefits, vacation days, days off, coffee breaks, chance for promotion with more freedom, and retirement plans. In addition to money, these are our rewards and incentives for proper job performance. We earn these things in exchange for our labor. In the same way, children can earn rewards and incentives from their parents for appropriate and expected behavior. Which is better? "Katie, here is the concert ticket that you wanted. In exchange, I want you to promise to not take money out of my purse." Or "Katie, you can earn the money to go to the concert if you go through the month without any evidence of taking money from me or anyone else."

In the first instance, Katie has no incentive to stop stealing from mother and others; in the second she has definite incentive. This does not mean that Katie's stealing behavior will not still be tracked and monitored—it will be—it simply means that Katie can earn a positive incentive *as well as* avoiding a negative consequence for not stealing. We are literally telling the child that they can avoid the negative and choose the positive; they can avoid a negative consequence and earn a positive consequence.

Incentives must have meaning to the child in order to be effective. The reward must be something that is tied directly to the desired behavior and is something that the child wants or is willing to expend the effort to obtain.

"Billy! A whole week of positive reports of not back talking to teachers; let's go out for ice cream!" will not do. "Billy! A whole week of positive reports of not back talking to your teachers! Congratulations on your success. As we agreed, you can go to the football game tonight with your friends" is more like it. It is not enough to only attempt to deter negative, unwanted behavior; we must work to encourage positive, wanted behavior as well. As parents we want to consistently strengthen the occurrence of behavior we like and want to see repeated, and weaken and put the brakes on behavior we want to see ended. The best way to do this is to make it easy for the child to choose what psychologist Alan Kazdin calls the "positive opposite" of what they were choosing before. Incentives make that happen.

Rewards need not be expensive or elaborate to be effective.

"Jimmy! You did a great job bundling up all the newspapers. Here is a Rolex watch. Enjoy!" is absurd. "Jimmy! You did a great job bundling up all the newspapers. I appreciate that," will do.

Wait a minute, what about the reward? Jimmy has his reward—my thanks and recognition for a job well done. This kind of reward is perfectly fine. In fact, most kids want praise and recognition from their parents as much or more than any tangible reward.

PRAISE

Praise is the single most effective way to reward positive behavior and to reinforce the likelihood of its being repeated. If you want your child (or your spouse, coworker, relative, or friend) to repeat a positive behavior that you like, then praise him for it. This is true whether someone is two years old, or ninety-two years old.

Praise is best when it is *limited, specific,* and *given sincerely.* This is as it should be because it is reflective of how things are in the larger world. Our boss doesn't praise us to the skies every morning when we show up for work on time. However, she may comment on it and we may have a written notice in our evaluation that we are punctual. That tends to make us want to be punctual.

Nor do you want to praise any and every behavior that your child is capable of doing ("Hey, great breathing today, keep it up!"). But you do want to take notice of and praise a positive behavior that the child is establishing: "I noticed that as soon as you came home from school you fed the dog. That's cool."

Think about the teacher at your child's school whom the kids will walk on hot coals to please. Not only does that teacher tend to set high standards, but she also tends to consistently praise students for every achievement connected to those standards. The teacher's praise is limited to the issue of schoolwork, is specific to what she found praiseworthy, and is given sincerely because he or she wants to see the behavior repeated: "Jonathan, your science project was turned in right on time. Excellent. I really like the way you illustrated the chambers of the heart. I enjoy reading your reports and it is a pleasure to have you in class. Very fine work, indeed."

As in the example, in order for praise to be effective, you need to limit your praise to the circumstance at hand, and sincerely and specifically say what it is that you appreciate or admire that the child has done. Don't say, "Good job on the kitchen"; instead say what you like and appreciate: "I see that you have all of the dishes washed and put away, the counters cleaned, and the floor swept—very nicely done. I appreciate your having it all done before we need to leave for the game. It is a pleasure to be able to rely on you."

Avoid Mixing Praise with Criticism

When you praise, withhold criticism. "I see that you have all of the dishes washed and put away, the counters cleaned, and the floor swept—very nicely done. I just wish you hadn't waited until almost game time to start doing it. Let's see if you can do better next time, okay?" Right. In this instance, your child will very likely remember the criticism and ignore the praise. The probable result is that the next time you want the kitchen cleaned, she will think, "Why should I? All I get is criticized for it."

Mixing Constructive Criticism with Feedback

There is nothing wrong with criticism. Often it is how we learn to do better. However, the most useless criticism for anyone is stinging criticism given when no corrective action can be taken: "Now, why did you leave your bike outside unlocked? Don't you realize how easy it is for someone to steal it? That was a damn fool thing to do."

Feedback, on the other hand, is a process for giving useful information. You can help your child do better consistently by combining useful information with feedback: "You left your bike outside unlocked and someone stole it. That was an unfortunate choice on your part. If the police recover your bike, or you use your savings to buy another one, get a secure lock or bring the bike into the house after you ride it." In this case, you're criticizing the child's behavior choice—not the child—and you are giving useful information about how he can do better, which will give you an opportunity to praise him in the future.

Praise in public for all to hear; give constructive criticism in private for only one to hear. Never criticize your child in front of an audience. If you do the kid will likely play to the audience in order to save face. Instead, wait for a time when you are alone and away from the situation. Then calmly say what you like, and what you do not; what you want to see more of, and what you want to see less of. Praise with a good deal more frequency than you give criticism.

Praise the character traits or behavior patterns you want to see more frequently. The best way to do this is to describe the specific positive behavior you are aware of or see: "You made some very intelligent and mature choices about not going into the store with someone who has a history of shoplifting." "I appreciate your willingness to jump right in and help us with the yard work. Your work helped us finish much faster." "You are a very kind and thoughtful person to volunteer your time to read to the kids at the library."

Combine Praise with Physical Affection

Another thing you can do that will reinforce your praise is to combine it with expressions of physical affection. As you praise your child, give her a hug, or a kiss, or both. If you can't hug or kiss, you can put a hand on her shoulder, or even just make eye contact.

COMBINE PRAISE WITH FORMAL REWARDS AND INCENTIVES

Praise should be the primary way in which we seek to reinforce positive behavior, but it is not the only way. Giving your child formal rewards and incentives for positive behavior is a good way, too.

Many parents bristle at the idea of offering their misbehaving kids rewards and incentives for proper behavior—as well they should. It is useless and counterproductive to attempt to stop negative behavior with positive rewards. This tactic doesn't work and is psychologically destructive to both the parent and the child. Don't do it.

Instead, use positive rewards to reinforce positive behavior. There is a world of difference between the two. Formal rewards and incentives are very effective in increasing *positive* behavior. They are totally ineffective in decreasing *negative* behavior, so should never be used for that purpose. Consider the difference between a movie pass and a movie ticket.

It's Saturday morning and Sam wants to study for a test that could lead to a job promotion. His eleven-year-old son has been an obnoxious hellion all morning. Sam gives his son the money for a movie ticket so he can get him out of his hair for a few hours.

Good Parent Sam has consequently done nothing more than reinforce his son's obnoxious behavior, because it has led to a free movie. The unwitting message to his son is that the next time he wants to attend a movie, all he has to do is act up. He has learned the power of coercion cloaked in the art of extortion.

Rosa's twelve-year-old son has been trustworthy and responsible by getting all of his point charts for the week. She rewards him by giving him a weekly movie pass.

See the difference? The first example is a bribe. The second is an earned reward. A bribe is never earned. A reward must be.

A parent can give spontaneous rewards in addition to earned ones. Say, "Because you've been so helpful around the house, let's stop for a banana split." Not, "If you'll stop screaming in my ear while I'm driving, I'll buy you a damn banana split!"

Children learn what we teach them. When we reward them, even inadvertently, for negative behavior, they are very likely to repeat it. When we deliberately reward them for positive behavior, they will repeat that as well. That is the way behavior works.

We have all made the mistake of rewarding negative behavior with positive rewards. You've done it, our parents have done it, and I have certainly done it. One reason is because it can require creativity to think of ways to reward both an older child and a younger child.

If my three-year-old can get through the candy section of the grocery store without throwing her usual tantrum, she may get a piece of sugarless candy when we get to the car. If she eats all of her dinner, she can have a dessert. And if she brushes her teeth, gets her jammies on, and into bed without a fuss, I'll come in and read her a story. My eleven-year-old isn't likely to be too thrilled when I come in to read her a bedtime story. However if she gets to bed on time I will tape her favorite late night show so she can watch it the next day.

Ask your child what he or she would find appealing as a possible reward. For most children, this will involve either time or money, such as extra spending money or the freedom to go and do something special. For younger children this will likely involve having special time with the parents or friends to do or have something special.

KINDS OF REWARDS

There are at least four categories of rewards that can be used to help change children's behavior: social, activity, material, and unconditional. Rewards can be given daily, weekly, or at the moment.

Social Rewards

Social rewards certainly include praise and recognition, but they also include spending quality and fun time together with other people, including parents. In addition to spending time with friends and other peers, have the child spend time with you. Going on a picnic, playing a game, and going out to dinner and a movie are all good ways to reward the child's positive behavior.

Activity Rewards

Activity rewards are designed to make the child's free time contingent upon the positive use of her scheduled time. If she has used her school time appropriately and completed her household chores, then she should have free time in the evening, on weekends, and during vacation time for pleasurable activities: playing video games, watching TV, visiting friends, or doing as she pleases. The critical link is that extra free time be first earned, not first given.

- Every time you complete all of your homework, you can do as you please until bedtime.
- When you have finished all of your chores, you can go out with your friends.

- For every task you complete, you can earn an extra twenty minutes on your computer or cell phone.

Material Rewards

As the name implies, material rewards are given in the form of money or things that cost money. We can give our kids money or an allowance and require nothing more from them than that they continue to draw breath, or we can make the giving of money conditional upon their positive behavior. Certainly, children can do extra chores around the house, work in your business if they are old enough, or secure a part-time job, such as a paper route, to earn money. But if we want to use money as a motivator, use it on a contractual basis: When this happens, that will happen.

- When you can pull your overall marks up one grade point, I'll go half way with you on a skateboard we choose together.
- If you complete this list of extra chores, and after I've checked to make sure they are done satisfactorily, I'll pay you $10 for each one.
- If you watch your little sister tonight while your mom and I go out, we'll pay the minimum wage.

It is perfectly all right to reward money that goes directly into a kid's checking account or savings account. Many children learn quickly how to manage their spending habits when they must rely on a bank account to make purchases. You can also give money for birthdays and holidays or for other special purposes. Just be sure that your child has ample opportunity to earn money as well.

Unconditional Rewards

Unconditional rewards are the most fun to give and to receive. You can give them for general, positive behavior that you want to see repeated. Since your child never knows when he or she will receive one, these rewards tend to be very reinforcing.

- "Hey, you guys were so helpful at the family barbecue I thought we'd have your friends over next weekend for another one."
- "You made Black Belt rank and I am very proud of you. I'd like to have your certificate framed and put up in the living room."
- "I'm so pleased with your willingness to share the computer time with your brother and sister. Let's get that upgrade that you wanted."

It is fine to use more than one type of reward, such as mixing praise with a material reward. It is also a good idea to keep a mental note of what kind of reward your child seems to respond to most consistently, and to use that.

THIRTEEN WAYS TO SHOW LOVE AND AFFECTION

1. Praise

Praise is the single most powerful way to encourage and support positive behavior. If you want to see a child repeat a certain behavior, praise him for it. Praising means that you love enough to do it. If your child does not respond well to praise, use acknowledgment.

2. Acknowledgment

To acknowledge means to recognize what is in a positive way. Compliments are good ways to acknowledge your child: "Wow, I like that haircut. That looks good." You can also acknowledge without putting a positive spin on it: "I see you got your math assignment done." Acknowledgment means I've taken notice because I care so much about you.

3. Expressions of Affection

Some parents say "I love you" easily and often; others find it difficult or awkward. But every child needs to hear his or her parents say it, preferably at least once a day. The same is true of hugs and kisses: Some kids (and parents) who would be embarrassed with a sugary "I love you" can get the same message with a kiss or hug.

4. Touch

A light touch on the shoulder or the hand can have a calming and soothing effect, and also convey the message "I love you." Interestingly, research has found that people are almost universally more likely to be cooperative and helpful to others when they are touched than when they are not. Touch is a powerful device for making emotional contact.

5. Listening with Empathy

Listen accurately and with compassion when children are in distress. Listen to their words, and then give voice to the underlying feelings. Listen with deep-seated concern, with the same wounded heart. Listening in this manner is a wonderful way to express your love.

6. Spending Time Together

Spending time as a family and separately with each child in the family gives families a strength and solidarity that is vital. Spend time with your child going on short trips, attending religious services, seeing places of interest, attending sporting or cultural events, or going out for planned and unplanned activities. Even if you must schedule the time or sacrifice your own time, it is important that you follow this practice as a means of expressing your love to your child.

7. Doing Things Together

There are many things you can do together with your child involving teamwork or partnership that results in loving fellowship. Pray or meditate together, restore or build something, exercise together, take music or sports lessons, volunteer together, attend or be a helper at your child's school play, sporting event, recital, or function—the choices are unlimited.

8. Teaching

Remember when you read stories to your toddler? Remember when you helped with their spelling words, or taught them to ride bikes or swim? Teaching often goes by the wayside when kids become older and more independent. You can teach anything you know that interests your child as well. Spending time teaching your child how to build a boat, bake, sew, throw a football, or apply a scripture lesson can all be very good ways to express your love to your child.

9. Family Circle

Choose a time when all family members are home and are relaxed. Have a short meeting wherein one person speaks at a time and says positive things about other family members—things they appreciate or wish to praise. This will increase the odds of that person repeating the positive behavior, and it builds family cohesion and togetherness. Doing this while the family is having dinner at the table is a great idea.

10. Caring Days/Love Days

Choose a day to give your child your undivided attention. This is a Valentine's Day for your child. Send him or her a gift or flowers; give extra hugs, kisses, and I-love-you expressions. Do something with your child that she especially likes to do. Go fishing, attend a rock concert, go on a hike, ride bikes, run around on the playground, go shopping, and so on. Spend the entire day being out and about and listening to her talk and enjoying her company. Rotate the love day to include every member of the family.

11. Thank-You-Grams/Love Grams

Write notes that you leave out where your child will find them—by his bed or on the kitchen table. A written note carries more weight than a quick "thank you" or "I love you, guys" tossed over your shoulder as you run out the door. The Thank-You-Gram recognizes your child for something he has done that has pleased you. The Love Gram is an expression of affection and/ or recognition. You can combine the two or use one or the other. For example, "I saw how hard you worked on the project today. I just wanted to say I think you're a great kid. I love you. Dad."

12. Laughter

Humor makes the heart feel light and the day go easier. Share jokes and stories with your child. A little gentle teasing can build intimacy and express love. Have some fun with your child. Do things together as a family that will induce laughter: watch a silly movie, play a goofy game, have a water balloon or snowball fight. When you can laugh together, your love will shine.

13. Play

Play is the language of childhood. Play is how children express themselves. Encourage your child to spend time in play either by themselves or with peers. It is also very important that you spend time playing with your child from a very early age—there are entire therapies that teach parents of "difficult" children how to play and interact with their child. Happy, child-directed play with the parent tells the child I enjoy interacting with you and I love you just as you are.

INCENTIVES AND THE DEFIANT CHILD

One word of caution: for children who are *habitually involved* with tantruming, emotional meltdowns, manipulative, coercive behavior, and/or antisocial behavior, reward-based methods will likely prove to be a failure. They think they already have things as they wish them to be and are continually being reinforced for their behavior. To them, arguing, backtalk, fighting, destroying property, bullying, hurting others, lying, stealing, cheating, and going into an emotional tailspin are fun and worthwhile activities. They do not care if you are happy or unhappy with their behavior, and they don't need you to tell them how to live. They certainly don't see any need to "earn" freedom and privileges. They already have them.

Likewise, defiant kids who have weak emotional attachments to their parents may initially do poorly with a reward-based system. I very strongly urge you to *not* give up on these kids. They can and will respond with due diligence. First, take the five steps of the active consequence (chapter 4) as the first attempt to regain control. Once these antisocial behaviors have been brought under acceptable limits, you can start using reward-based incentives to help maintain the positive behavior.

When used consistently, rewards and incentives are powerful tools in changing the focus and direction of your child's behavior from negative to positive—no matter *how* negative the behavior may be. Just as a lathe is a tool used to "shape" material into a desired form, rewards and incentives can help you "shape" your child's behavior into the form you want to see. You just need to know how to use the tool properly to make it work for you to get the result that you want. And now you do.

II

Problem Behaviors and What to Do about Them

Part II provides suggested rules and consequences for problem behaviors. One or more of these consequences may work consistently in helping your child alter his or her behavior. If the effectiveness of the consequence begins to fade—or is plainly not working with your child—don't be afraid to try another. You can make a Rules Tracking Guide on which you list the rules, monitor compliance, and record progress.

The problem behaviors covered in this section are:

- Arguing
- Backtalk
- Bullying
- Cheating
- Chore completion
- Fighting
- Friends
- Information technology
- Lying
- Manners
- School assignments and homework
- Sibling fighting
- Stealing
- Swearing
- Television and video games

- Truancy and misbehavior in school
- Whereabouts and curfews

Chapter Ten

Arguing

Sample consequence rule: Never argue; discuss.
Natural consequence: People do not want to be around the child because he/she is unpleasant, objectionable, and tiresome.
Logical consequence: When the child begins to argue, do not talk to him/her and walk away. Parents will take away privileges or deny requests.
Active consequences: Argument deflectors, the sponge, broken record, the wall, and clouding (see below for skills).

Parent educator Gregory Bodenhamer asks how many times you have won an argument with another person. How many times has the person suddenly stopped with a look of enlightened astonishment crossing his face and said, "You know, you're right! I never thought of those things. I don't know how I could have been so wrong! I want to thank you for your profound wisdom and for pointing out the error of my ways. From now on I'll always listen to you." Now think, how many times have you won an argument with a child? When pigs fly.

Arguments are verbal combat. They are not designed to persuade with reasoned discourse, rather they are designed to wear down an opponent. Arguing is by its very nature harmful and unproductive. It destroys relationships. Even when you think you win, you lose. You can't win an argument with anyone. You can only engage in one, going around in circles.

Kids see arguments as a wonderful diversion. They may try to get you into an angry argument about what a lousy parent you are: You are so unfair, you never listen to their side of things, you're always picking on them, you never let them have any fun, they're old enough to choose for themselves, and so on. If they are successful in getting your goat they can divert you from the issue at hand and on to something else—often something completely unrelated to the topic at hand.

Here is the key to "winning" an argument with a child: Never argue. Yeah, but that is easy to say and hard to do, especially when the kid is yelling and in your face. That's right, it is hard to avoid arguing right back and not return anger with anger. Anger begets anger. And arguing is the blood brother of anger. To learn how to avoid and deflect arguments, you need practice using the right tools.

First, learn to control anger. There are any number of good books on the subject and therapy programs. If you can't control anger you can kiss any hope of avoiding arguments with your child goodbye.

Second, understand what arguing is: raising your voice, using insults and putdowns, being unwilling to let the other person speak and to listen, and repeating the same words again and again—only louder. Arguing is also denying that what the other person is saying is true or has any merit. Arguing is the absence of reasoned discussion. It is communication with malice.

Third, do not let your child bait you into an argument. Children are frequently masters at throwing out emotional hooks and reeling their parents into an argument. Emotional hooks usually begin with the word "you."

- You never let me do anything!
- You never listen to what I have to say!
- You and Dad are always against me!

Children also employ the insincere question:

- "What's the matter, Dad? Don't you trust me?"
- "Why is it that everything I say and do is wrong?"
- "Don't you love me?"

And the time-honored manipulative con of sidetracking:

- "All my friends are doing it! Their parents trust them. They're cool. They don't care how late their kids stay out."
- "Well, if I don't get to go, how come I have to keep my room clean?"
- "If you hadn't have married Jim, I wouldn't want to be out late with my friends."

What is the solution? Be prepared for arguments with argument deflectors, a way to short-circuit arguments. You "deflect" the argument by never letting it start.

ARGUMENT DEFLECTORS

There are any number of words or phrases that can be used as argument deflectors. Gregory Bodenhamer suggests the use of the words "regardless" and "nevertheless." If you like a touch of formality, there is "be that as it may," "notwithstanding," "in any event," or "nonetheless." If you wish to address the issue more directly, there is "that is not the point," "even so," "just the same," or "even though you may think/believe otherwise." They work like this:

- "Regardless of how late your friends can stay out, be home by dark."
- "Regardless if you believe it's not fair, finish your chores now."
- "Nevertheless, you cannot attend an R-rated movie."
- "Nevertheless, I need forty-eight hours' notice before you can go to a sleepover."
- "Be that as it may, the rule stands."
- "Even though you may think otherwise, I will never buy you a motor-bike."

The Sponge

The sponge, another technique from Gregory Bodenhamer, unemotionally soaks up the argument with these phrases: "Uh huh." "I hear you." "You already said that. Was there anything else?"

The Broken Record

If your child continues to argue after using the argument deflectors, try the broken record. Simply repeat the consequence rule or your brief explanation—not ad nauseam, once or twice should do. Say it once and then if needed repeat the same words again. What is the last thing that the child hears? The rule or the explanation. If your child is too young to understand words like "regardless" or phrases like "that is not the point," using the sponge or the broken record will work just as well to deter arguments.

- "The rule is always be where I can see you while we are in the store."
- "The rule is attend every after school music lesson."
- "This is against our family values for someone your age."
- "I understand you don't like it, and you'll need to babysit your brother tonight."

The Wall

Still arguing? Try this exercise. Pick any wall in your house. Pull the blinds so that the neighbors won't see you. Now walk up to the wall and start to argue. Were you able to persuade the wall to give in? To change its mind? I call this technique "The Wall." When your child continues to argue with you after you have tried these other skills, use the wall. Simply stand there and say nothing. Retreat into stony silence. Walk away. Occupy yourself with something else, because you are done with the child's rudeness. If need be, and if it is safe for your child to be alone for a few minutes, lock yourself in the bathroom. Silence makes most people uncomfortable, and it will drive a habitually arguing child nuts. It's very effective.

Now, what if you're afraid of the arguing child? You've used the wall and locked yourself in the bathroom for two or three minutes, but you're afraid your child will beat on the door, or trash the house. Take a cell phone with you before you go so that you can call for help if things get out of hand.

CLOUDING

Somewhat related to argument deflectors is clouding. Here you simply agree with some small aspect of what the child has said before you dismiss it or totally disagree.

- "Yes, I agree we do have strict rules."
- "I agree. Your friend's parents give them more freedom."
- "That's right. You're not a little kid anymore."

This technique throws the arguing kid off balance. The last thing he expects you to do is to agree with him. He expects you to argue. Instead, you are simply acknowledging the facts: yes, it really is Tuesday, and he has had a week to finish an uncompleted English assignment due tomorrow. You're not arguing about whether or not it's stupid and if he really has to do it.

- "Yes, I agree we have strict rules about completing homework assignments before they are due. I agree that your friend's parents give them more freedom about completing assignments and turning them in late, and we do not."
- "That's right, you're not a little kid anymore, and I shouldn't have to remind you, but I do because you are not yet self-directed about doing your homework."
- "You're absolutely right. You can handle it. I shouldn't have to be networking with your teacher—and I will network until you can handle your schoolwork consistently."

Like the others, clouding is a very effective tool to divert arguments.

IF THEY HAVE A VALID POINT

Now what do you do if you would be willing to cut the kid some slack? Maybe they do have a point or you do want to consider at least some of what she wants. First, repeat the rule about never arguing but discussing. This signals to the child that you would be willing to seek common ground. Next say, "I'm willing to discuss this with you, but I will not argue with you. What would you like to do?"

What if the child keeps arguing only because she wants the last word? Kids want the last word as a means of saving face. Let them have it. You have already "won" the argument by not engaging in it.

What if the child has been firing barbed arrows at you and you don't feel like discussing anything with her? In that case, unemotionally ask her about her intentions: "Did you want me to know how you feel about me, or did you want to try and resolve the problem?" You've left the door wide open for the child to take the mature stance of engaging in some active problem solving with you. Or she can continue to berate you and get—nothing.

Most kids—just like adults—repeat behavior they think is in their own best interest. When parents use these tools consistently, kids learn very quickly that arguing is not in their own best interest. Then they stop doing it.

Arguing immediately puts you in a one-down position with your child. Never argue, and you'll never fear having to confront your child.

Chapter Eleven

Backtalk

Sample consequence rules: Never speak to me with disrespect. Never speak to any adult in authority with disrespect. Never use rude gestures when speaking to someone.

Natural consequence: People do not want to be around the child because they find them to be unpleasant, objectionable, and tiresome.

Logical consequence: For young children, ignore the backtalk. For older children, use time-out or loss of privileges related to the backtalk such as being denied permission for an activity.

Active consequences: Argument deflectors: the sponge, clouding, the wall (see Arguing).

Backtalk in children has a number of similarities to arguing, but is not the same behavior. Backtalk is any child response to an adult in authority—such as the parent, a teacher, or caregiver—given in a disrespectful manner. Backtalk often comes just *before* an argument. It is the death-defying sighs, the eye-rolls, the fingernails-on-blackboard whining, the venomous stare, the sneering, muttering sarcasm, or the snide remark. Like these: "You don't know everything." "Yeah, yeah . . . anything you say." "I don't have to listen to you." "Big deal, who cares?" "Whatever." "Chill, man!" and "Make me." Sometimes in backtalk children use rude gestures to emphasize their point. You know the ones—with little kids, the tongue stick-out, older kids the middle finger salute, the presentation of the backside, and other more imaginative gestures.

Backtalk is learned. If a child learns through experience that it is acceptable to backtalk parents, they will extrapolate from this experience to believe it is acceptable to backtalk their teachers, caregivers, grandparents, and others—essentially any adult with authority over them. It is not that the child has learned that backtalk is what adults *want*; it is that they have gotten away with it more than once and now it is *okay* to do.

WHERE DO KIDS LEARN BACKTALK?

Where do kids learn this rude, vulgar behavior? We don't have to look far. Children imitate other children. Cartoons and TV situation comedies are loaded with smart and foulmouthed children who routinely backtalk adults to the accompaniment of laugh tracks. Children regularly witness adults who backtalk each other in a witless exchange of angry, impulsive behavior. Parents do it, siblings do it, the neighbors do it, strangers do it, and I have certainly done it too.

WHY DO KIDS USE BACKTALK?

Why do kids do it? Psychologists say that backtalk stems from a "sense of powerlessness and frustration." Many kids want to feel that they have the authority to make most, if not all, of their own choices and they don't like it when adults in authority tell them otherwise. Toddlers don't like it when they are told it is time to put away their toys and get ready for dinner. Young children don't appreciate being reminded to put on their boots before going out in a rainstorm. Older children don't want to get off their cell phones and start their homework. The natural result is to challenge the authority. Back-talk follows.

There are many ways to avoid the challenge and the conflict (see chapter 8). Backtalk is the absence of the skill of knowing how to avoid conflict and to express yourself in more appropriate ways.

BACKTALK: THE PROBLEM

How do you know that backtalk is a serious problem?

- Your child does not stop backtalk when told to do so
- The backtalk is increasing in frequency and intensity
- The backtalk is ruining your relationship
- Other people are complaining or are concerned about the child's backtalk
- The child is using backtalk as a tool to annoy or attack others

Backtalk in children is not cute or funny. Like arguing it is harmful and unproductive. It destroys relationships. It teaches children to be rude and manipulative. But you don't have to tolerate it or hope they outgrow it. You can end backtalk. Use these steps to end backtalk and then be consistent in following through with them until backtalk is a thing of the past.

FOUR STEPS:

STEP 1: CALL OUT BACKTALK ON THE SPOT

When you first hear backtalk, call your child on it. "Jacob, do not backtalk, now or ever. Your words are disrespectful and will not be tolerated. Speak to me in a manner that will make me want to listen." If the child continues to backtalk, use the sponge: "Uh huh. You already said that. Anything else?" You can also use clouding: "You may be right, son. I may not know everything. But I do know that your backtalk will never get you anything from me." Continue on to step two.

STEP 2: REFUSE TO ENGAGE

"When you use backtalk, I will not engage in a struggle with you. When you use appropriate words I will listen to what you have to say. If you want to discuss things in a calm manner, let's do so." If the child refuses the invitation and continues to backtalk, go to step three.

STEP 3: IMPOSE A CONSEQUENCE

"I have told you to never backtalk. There is a consequence for backtalk, and here it is." Impose the consequence—time-out, loss of freedom or a privilege, being denied permission for an activity, a work detail, and the like. At this step put up your palm as a signal that you are now done. Use "The Wall" and walk away in silence.

STEP 4: PRAISE AND REWARD THE POSITIVE OPPOSITE OF BACKTALK

When the child is following the consequence rule about backtalk, offer them praise and small rewards. "Jenny, thank you for listening while I was talking. I appreciate that you didn't backtalk—super effort." "Chrissie, I know you didn't like my answer, but you didn't backtalk. I've noticed that you've been trying hard all week to curb backtalk. That is great. Now, do you still want to go to the movies with Karen? I will be happy to drive the two of you."

The parents in the above examples make turning aside backtalk in their children look easy. It will not be easy until you get the hang of using the four steps and your child is responding without backtalk. While you practice, here are four things to keep in mind.

- Stay calm: The argument deflector techniques will work just as well for backtalk. They will not work worth a hoot if your child uses backtalk and you respond in anger. Backtalk is an attention-seeking behavior. Attention-seeking works especially well if you respond with flaming hot words back to the child—"You can't talk to me like that, you little @#$%^!"— with the argument quick on its heels. If you need help staying calm, raise your palm as a signal that you will not engage and then walk away from the child using "The Wall" technique and then give yourself a relaxing time-out.
- Be consistent: Make a mental commitment to use these deterrent skills every time your child engages in backtalk. You are training the child not to use backtalk, and consistency in application is the key to establishing any new positive behavior.
- Do not fire back: Do not model the very same negative behavior that you want to eliminate. Do not echo the child's whining, do not sigh loudly, eye roll, sneer, or try to be clever with acid sarcasm or snide remarks. Be the adult and not the child.
- Try again: Just as you may need to try again while learning the skills, have your child try again, too. You can tell the child, "Try again, Patrick. Ask for what you want without whining and eye rolling." When the child is able to gain what they want from the parent without backtalk, they learn quickly that it is to their advantage to eliminate backtalk.

Eliminating backtalk teaches children to engage with adult authority figures in a calm and respectful manner. They learn that adults reciprocate with calmness and due respect, and that they then often have a far easier time interacting with and gaining things from adults. Eliminating backtalk also increases the positive regard between parent and child and makes for a happier home. What a marvelous outcome.

Chapter Twelve

Bullying

Sample consequence rule: Never bully anyone at any time for any reason.
Natural consequence: The child earns a reputation as a thug.
Logical consequences: The child will receive sanctions from parents and at school and other places for bullying; he may be criminally charged for harassment, intimidation, menacing, stalking, and/or assault.
Active consequences: Intercession, networking, tracking, monitoring, and supervising.

Children bully other children because they believe they can do so. They then do it with enough frequency and intensity so that not only is this behavior a serious problem for them but for their victims. When you read and hear about bullying, this is something that is rarely acknowledged: Bullying is a *crime*. It should be treated like any other crime your child is capable of doing. That is, put a stop to it. Bullying behavior is an antisocial behavior that can have serious consequences far beyond the bullying behavior itself. Children who are habitually bullied can suffer deep emotional scars and there have been instances where children pursued suicide or even lethal retaliation.

THE FOUR CHARACTERISTICS OF BULLYING

1. Bullying is *intentional*. Bullies mean what they say and behave the way that they choose. There are no "accidents" in bullying, or mere thoughtless action. Bullies mean to cause harm or pain. They do it because they enjoy doing it.
2. Bullying is *repetitive*. There are no one-time bullies. When a child bullies another child they will repeat that behavior until they are

forced to do otherwise. The bully wagers that the victim will not tell or resist and often they are right.

3. Bullying is *hurtful*. Bullying is physical and/or emotional abuse. Children are beaten. They are tormented. They are frightened. They are marginalized. They are abused in ways that no one should ever be.
4. Bullying is *wrong*. Bullying is a moral offense. Anytime there is an imbalance of power between two people—because of age, strength, social status, gender, race, ethnicity, religion, appearance, or preference—and one person seeks to use imbalance as a power position over another, that is wrong; and that is the essence of bullying.

PUTTING A STOP TO BULLYING

As a parent, you should seek to put a stop to your child's bullying the first time that you are made aware of it. When you have reports, witnesses, or evidence of bullying by your child this is what you do.

Networking

Find out when and how often the child is doing it. Use your network to ask parents, teachers, counselors, clergy, child-care workers, friends, relatives, and anyone else who has consistent contact with your child, if they have knowledge of your child bullying another child by words or actions. You want to know what happened and how often it has happened. If the child has engaged in bullying on one occasion or more than several, have a "Straight Talk" session with the child. In your own words, explain to them that bullying is intentional, repetitive, hurtful, and wrong—and will not be tolerated. Logical consequences for bullying include: making apologies, returning any stolen items, confiscating items such as computers, cell phones, or other devices that may have been used in bullying, and having the child inform others of what they did and how they plan not to repeat the behavior.

If the bullying behavior has been more frequent or intense, your consequences need to be more frequent and intense. At this level active consequences are the best way.

Intercession

Most schools now have anti-bullying programs in place. Children are encouraged to tell and to seek help if they have a problem with bullying. Adult mentors are sometimes trained to approach and work with both bullying offenders and victims. Find out what your child's school has to offer. If the school does not offer what you need, seek help from organizations such as the Boys and Girls Club, religious centers, charitable groups, or contact children's mental health agencies for referrals for anti-bullying therapy services. If the child is referred to the police and placed on probation by the court, accept this consequence, as hard as that may be for you. The community has a stake in ending your child's bullying behavior. The intent of childhood probation is not incarceration but rehabilitation—even for young children.

Seek therapy if the bullying child has experienced emotional trauma. Frequently bullies are unhappy children who seek to take out their distress on others. Often bullies have been bullied themselves or are being bullied. Bullies often have learning difficulties in school and may have been tormented or marginalized by their peers. All of these things can be repaired with due diligence.

Tracking

Bullies often find it hard to give it up. After all, bullying gives them a certain exalted social status or positive regard that they may not otherwise enjoy; and then too they have convinced themselves that it's fun. As the parent of a bully, you want to be certain that the child is really applying themselves to changing their behavior. Keep a tracking sheet of the bullying behavior. Look to see how often the child is engaging in the behavior by reports or by witness, and then consequence accordingly.

Monitoring

Know where the child is, who they are with, and what they are likely doing. If the child is more likely to bully others when they are with certain friends or associates, or in certain locations—such as school—then limit free access to those children or locations. The child cannot be unattended at the bus stop, the playground, a friend's home, movie theater, the mall, the park, the arcade, the pool, and so on. Give the child a small amount of freedom and then shape the desired non-bullying behavior. Follow the positive non-bullying behavior with lifting of freedom restrictions and in a point system with positive rewards for positive behavior.

Supervision

If the child is not making headway in altering their bullying behavior, then provide responsible adult supervision. Place the child on a level system. If the level system is only effective as long as it is in place, then provide eyeball supervision with a limited amount of freedom. Go with the child to school one day and sit with them in class. Escort them to the playground, the friend's home, movie theater, mall, park, arcade, pool, and so on. The child cannot bully when an adult authority is supervising and is willing to follow through. At some point—and usually the point is reached quickly—the child will have the insight that it is to his advantage to not bully others. Then they stop doing it.

HELPING THE CHILD WHO IS THE VICTIM OF BULLYING

As we have described, the parent can do any number of things to stop bullying behavior. You can also enlist a host of people to help put an end to bullying. Now, what do you do if your child is not the bully, but the victim of the bully?

Certainly it is wise to teach the child—however young they may be—to tell a trusted adult that they are being bullied. However, children are frequently told to ignore taunts and malicious teasing, avoid the bully, refuse to be afraid, or "be better" than the bully. They are also sometimes told to "stick up" for themselves and to fight back; or to "meet fire with fire," and to find ways to extract revenge on the bully by bullying them. These are all well-intended measures; they rarely work and often make things worse for the victim.

What *does* work is a partnership between the parent and child to eliminate bullying from the child's life, and to teach the child their own anti-bullying skills. This is what is needed:

Be the "trusted adult" that the child first tells that they are being bullied. Find out who, when, where, and what. Who is doing the bullying? When does the bullying happen? Where does it happen? And what is the child being bullied about? Then report what you know to people who have the authority to stop it.

Angel

Eight-year-old Angel has been withdrawn for the last month. She is sullen and moody. She cries easily. In the last week she has pretended to be sick in the mornings when she is expected to be preparing for school and pleads to stay home. The pediatrician can find nothing wrong with her. Angel's mother has asked Angel's best friend and her teacher if she is aware of anything at school that has been difficult lately for Angel. The best friend confides that a boy has been calling Angel a racial slur and blocking her path on the playground and in the hallways. The teacher says the boy has been warned to stop, but he has not been caught doing "anything concrete."

Because the mother has the skills to ask open questions and to listen with empathy, when she talks to Angel she is able to find out quickly what has happened at school with the bully. A month ago, the bully named Alan began calling her racial slurs, and told her to "Go back to Mexico." When she ignored his taunts he began confronting her on the playground and in the hallways with repeated insults and would squeeze her arm. He began to tell her that she was "dirty brown" and that she was a "stuck-up bitch" because she was so skilled in math. Angel began getting text messages from Alan that she showed to her mother. The most ominous one said, "Why don't you jump off a bridge and go to hell. Save me the trouble." Soon after, two of Alan's friends also began to harass her with taunts. Angel was afraid to tell anyone other than her best friend and now her mother. The mother praised Angel for her being strong and for telling her about the bullying.

The mother took her information to the school principal, who confronted Alan and Alan's parents. Alan denied the allegations but the principal and the parents did not believe him as there were witnesses, the text message sent from Alan's cell phone, and the parents' confirmation of Alan's previous bullying from prior school years. Alan was cited by the school resource officer and referred to the juvenile court, where he was mandated to make apologies to Angel and to complete an anti-bullying program. Angel returned to school with no long-term ill effects. As she progressed through school, she encouraged others who were being bullied to always tell and to seek help.

Angel did the right thing. She not only helped herself, she helped Alan. If your child is being bullied, they can do the same. Now, here are some specific skills that you can teach your child that will deter bullying.

Teaching Your Child to Deter Bullying

Bullies lie. Don't believe them. And never argue with them—there is nothing to argue about or discuss. Teach your child to assertively and calmly tell them:

1. "Do not speak to me like that."
2. "Do not touch me or my things."
3. "I will report you to a police officer."

Have the child use the Broken Record to repeat these three sentences. If the bully persists, have the child use Clouding:

- "You may be right. I may be a loser in your eyes. *And* I will report you to the police."
- "I agree. You could beat me up. *And* you'll be suspended and arrested."
- "That's right. You believe that you and your friends rule the school. *And* I have my own power."

Believe me bullies have not heard anything like this before from potential victims. It will come as a shock and confuse them. The easiest thing to do is to walk away and look for easier prey.

So what else?

If your child has the use of electronic gadgets have the child come to you immediately and show you any emails, text messages, or to listen to any recorded phone calls, that contain bullying messages, gossip, photographs, or threats. This is called cyberbullying, and is more common among girl bullies than boys. The same is true for any sent notes or letters. Keep this material as evidence to show to parents of bullies, or to the authorities. Tell the child who sent the material that you are aware of it, that you will report it to adults in authority, the server, the parents, and if need be, to the police.

If you have legitimate concerns that your child has been, or could become a victim of physical abuse the child needs to know how to defend themselves. This doesn't mean necessarily that the child must earn a black belt, but it does mean that the child has the physical means to deter aggression. Karate may be the answer—my fourteen-year-old daughter is a black belt and has the confidence and the communication skill to have never needed to use her skills. There are other martial arts such as aikido that do not inflict pain and injury, but quickly stop the aggressor.

Hopefully it will never come to that. But children who are prepared to deter bullying by confiding in a trusted adult and using assertiveness, argument deflectors, and self-defense are considerably less likely to be bullied and to have happier lives.

Chapter Thirteen

Cheating

Sample consequence rules: Never cheat. Always strive to do your best.
Natural consequence: Having a reputation as a cheater. The child is considered to be untrustworthy and unreliable.
Logical consequences: School consequences: failing tests, undertaking makeup and remedial work, and in-school detention. Having to repeat chore, task, or schoolwork assignments at home; loss of privileges and freedom.
Active consequences: Intercession, networking, tracking, monitoring, and supervision.

It is said that cheaters never prosper. Actually, sometimes they do. Some people become quite adept at cheating and have good success with it, unfortunately. Some cheaters think that it is the best they can do. In their own minds, it is an acceptable behavior.

Cheating frequently is a habit acquired during childhood. Children, just like everyone else, face competition and feel great social pressure to win. If they can't win at playing cards or at a game, then they may feel compelled to cheat their way to a win. When the stakes are higher—such as anxiety about failing a test and the ridicule that comes with it—children will sometimes resort to cheating as the lesser of two evils. If they believe that they can't meet their parent's expectations in performing a chore or task, they may cheat to win. Later still, when they believe that they *have* to cheat in order to have what they want; they can enter into a habit of cheating behavior. A few even become quite good at it.

TODAY'S WORLD

Nowadays, it is easy for children to cheat. There are calculators that will do your math operations for you. You can copy verbatim or plagiarize ideas from an essay on the Internet with ease. Someone will text you the answers during a test. Parents are so busy they frequently will accept the untrustworthy child's word for completed chores and tasks, and their version of events.

Arthur

Ten-year-old Arthur had a busy week. He had four major tasks to complete and he did them all. He had to write an essay about Abraham Lincoln. He had to complete a week's worth of math homework with long division. He had his weekly major chore of picking up all of the dog poop and putting it in the trash. And he walked five miles for donations to the breast cancer awareness program.

The next week Arthur was informed by his teacher that he had scored a 100 percent on his long division homework, but had failed completely on his math test. The teacher admired his essay on President Lincoln, but pointedly noted that the essay was one written by a well-known Lincoln scholar available on the Internet. The lawn service people complained to Arthur's parents that they could not mow the lawn what with all of the dog poop. And the breast cancer Walk-A-Thon supervisors informed Arthur's parents that he did indeed turn in his pledge card noting that he walked five miles, but no one ever saw him walking the route.

Arthur's confession to his parents included explanations. His older brother was quite skilled at long division and the homework was "just practice"; the Lincoln essay was everything he was going to write anyway; he thought the lawn service people could work around the dog poop; and he "really did" walk all five miles, they just didn't see him.

Arthur was a miserable failure as a cheater—not to mention as a liar. Arthur had cheated on his responsibilities numerous times. Arthur's parents required that he apologize to all concerned and do makeup work for his actions. However right and well-intended Arthur's parents' consequences indeed were, they did not get to the core of the problem of helping Arthur overcome his cheating habit.

Frequent cheating—like lying—is an acquired habit. In fact, lying and cheating are often twin problem behaviors; where you see one you usually see the other. Fortunately, like Arthur, most children are not very skilled at either one. Then why do they do it?

Children cheat because they fear failure and because, unfortunately, sometimes they can get by with it and avoid the anxiety and sense of loss of self-regard that comes with failure. So what can parents do if children are cheating on a regular basis?

INTERCESSION

Children know that cheating is morally wrong. There is no point in moralizing about it. What you can do is point out the one who cheats is hurt the most by cheating. Cheating robs you of the opportunity to succeed, but also to fail. Failure is as enlightening as success and is nothing more than a stepping-stone to success. There is nothing to fear in failure; true failure comes in not trying. Hold your head high, and try again. Do your best, and then strive to go beyond your best to achieve excellence.

Even though they may try again, it is true that some children feel anxious and discouraged when they feel incapable. If the child clearly is struggling to succeed in schoolwork, and is resorting to cheating to get by, then arrange for the intercession that will directly address the problem (see School Assignments and Homework). The same is true if the child cannot meet expectations for completing chores or other tasks (see Chore Completion). Do not accept flimsy excuses or rationalizations, but do be compassionate and proactive in assisting your child in overcoming cheating.

NETWORKING

If your child has a history of repeated cheating, network with the adults who spend time with your child on a regular basis. Inform teachers, coaches, child care workers, friends' parents, relatives, and others that you are working with your child on not cheating and would like to be informed if they see evidence of cheating. This intervention does two things: it gives you feedback that your child has cheated on schoolwork, during games, completing tasks, and at other times so that you can address it at home, and informs you when the child is choosing the positive opposite of not choosing to cheat, so that you can praise and reward them at home.

TRACKING

Examine the child's homework before they turn it in to the teacher. Ask them questions about the content of their work. If they cannot explain how they arrived at their answers to questions that is a sure indicator of cheating. If the child has written an essay or a report that has words or content that looks like it was written by someone with a college education, it probably was. And trust but verify that the child has indeed completed chores and tasks to a satisfactory standard.

MONITORING

You can take tracking a step further and monitor the child's whereabouts and activities. You can sit with the child at the kitchen table while they do their homework or do research on the computer. You can insist that they not have access to a cell phone while they are completing their homework to prevent friends from texting answers. And you can be close by when the child is completing chores or other tasks.

SUPERVISION

As noted, supervision is a more stringent form of monitoring; however, with cheating supervision should be the last resort. Arrange to have the child complete tests or other assigned work under the direct eyeball supervision of a trusted adult. Be with the child the entire time they are completing a chore or task and direct them to do it without cutting corners. After you do this a time or two, draw down to less direct supervision with periodic monitoring to completion. The intent here is to teach your child the futility of trying to cheat, and the pride that will come from not having to do so to be successful.

THE REALM OF POSSIBILITY

There is a realm of possibility for everyone. Every child and adult can be successful in the realm of possibility for them. That is not to say everyone can be the best, but everyone can do their best. It is not in the realm of possibility for everyone to become an astronaut, but everyone can reach the stars. Every child can learn, and grow, and achieve—and reach for their very own stars. Every child can dream and exceed their own expectations of what is possible for them. The realm of possibility for your child is here and now, and resides within them. And cheating plays no part in that.

Chapter Fourteen

Chore Completion

Sample consequence rule: Do all of your assigned chores every day that they are assigned.

Natural consequence: Child lives in a mess, with the resulting inconvenience and emotional upset.

Logical consequence: Choose any of the following to say to your child:

- For every chore of yours that I do, I will charge you a set amount of money.
- For every chore that I do for you, you'll do one for me.
- For every chore that you do not do, I will withhold one favor from you.
- For every chore that you do not do, you'll be assigned another in addition to the uncompleted chore.

Active consequences: Tracking, monitoring, and supervising.

Chores for kids usually fall into one of two categories: things that affect the child directly, or things that affect everyone in the family. Ideally, there should be a balance between the two. If everyone eats off the dishes, then everyone should have a turn in washing the dishes. If the child has a bedroom to herself, she should be responsible for its upkeep. If everyone uses the bathroom, then everyone should have a turn in scrubbing the toilet; likewise, if the child has a bathroom to himself, he needs to get acquainted with the toilet brush.

When your child is an adult and working in the "real world," will he be expected do only the work that involves him directly, or work that benefits the entire organization? At times it will be both. Chores are good training for the real world. The worker who knows and can perform multiple tasks in the workplace is usually the best worker.

Well, what's wrong with letting the kid be a kid? He'll have plenty of time to take on responsibilities when he becomes an adult. Think for a moment about the most irresponsible adult you know. This person is in and out of jobs, relationships, and trouble. Now think, how good do you think this person was at doing chores as a child? Not very. And likely even today this person relies upon others to clean up every mess that he leaves. Doing chores as a child gives rise to the responsible adult.

Further, kids with weak attachments to the family often find that when they are relied upon in a positive way by having chores, their feeling of attachment to the family and their sense of self-worth increase. Attachment also has the side benefit of decreasing resistance to doing chores.

Chores should be necessary, fair and reasonable, clearly understood, enforceable, and age appropriate—just like rules. In fact, you can examine the prospective chore assignment with the same perspective used in constructing rules (see chapter 2). It is a good idea to ask each family member which chore—if any—he or she might want to do. Some kids like chopping firewood or dusting the furniture. It is also a good idea to rotate responsibility for chore completion—especially for the most odious chores. Young children cannot be expected to do complex chores, but can be responsible for simple chores—such as putting away their toys and clean clothes, making their bed, bringing in the newspaper or setting the table, or feeding their goldfish or hamster. One thing you do not want is that the child have no chores, or to do it yourself because it is just easier that way. Everybody is somebody, and everybody can contribute.

Once you have settled on the chores you want your child to do, the best way to ensure their completion is having chores done on a schedule. Just as you brush your teeth in the morning on a regular routine, so should your child be expected to complete chores on a regular routine.

A written chore list is better than an oral commitment. It is also a good idea to run through *in detail* what you want your child to do and when it is to be done. Show your child, "This is what I mean by a 'clean' room; mowing the lawn means thus and so on; preparing the dishwasher involves doing this." This procedure will help prevent arguments and upset feelings later over what standard is being used.

For example, if you want the bathroom cleaned you might write out the standards like this: Before 9:00 am every Saturday morning, clean the entire bathroom. Find the cleansers under the sink. Swish a cap full of the toilet cleaner into the bowl and then brush the sides, the base, and the rim with the toilet brush until they are spotless. Do the same to the sink and tub with the tub and tile cleanser. Pick up all the soiled towels and place them in the hamper. Find fresh towels in the closet and put them on the racks. Sweep the floor and empty the trash can.

NATURAL CONSEQUENCES

Natural consequences can be used to enforce chore completion. If you don't have to look at a mess, perhaps you can live with it. You can shut the child's bedroom door and walk on. For example, on washday when the underwear is still on the bedroom floor—so be it. If the child wants clean underwear, she can make other arrangements—or be sure and have them in the hamper on the next washday. If the child leaves their toys scattered around the house, they cannot readily find the toy they want. If the child doesn't make their bed, then the bed is uncomfortable that evening before they get in bed. No matter how it goes, your child is making the choice and has the natural consequence.

LOGICAL CONSEQUENCES

Logical consequences can be devised for the child to experience and can likewise be used to enforce chore completion. Look for the consequences that are most consistently effective and logically related. Confiscation and taking away favors/privileges are two good logical consequences to use. For example, if the child flatly refuses to keep his room clean, then confiscate the room or objects in the room. Start by removing the bedroom door. If the defiance persists, confiscate items in the room until the child decides it is to his advantage to comply with keeping the room clean, or padlock the bedroom for a day or two except for bedtime. He can earn back confiscated items—or use of the bedroom for the day—for every day the room is clean to established standards. Conversely, you can take away privileges or favors until the child determines that he can do chores after all.

ACTIVE CONSEQUENCES

Active consequences are the most useful with the semi-responsible and the irresponsible child. You'll want to employ the active consequences of tracking, monitoring, and supervision. Make sure that you get your child started on the chore with clear instructions, and then track her progress and the chore's completion periodically (every ten minutes or so). Or you may need to provide supervision by being present the entire time the child is working.

For the kid who does the chore but is a real slug, consider using a timer. Have one timer set for her and another one for you (some kids will try to set back time). If your child can't finish the chore in a reasonable time, she can have a second chore. However, be sure to praise her for successfully completing the chore on time when that happens, and offer an incentive for consistent success. For example, if she completes the chores well and on time four times in a row, give her a break from doing the chore the fifth time. When you have consistent compliance, move back down to a milder consequence for not completing the chore on time or none at all.

WORKING TOGETHER

For infrequent work chores, such as cleaning the gutters, planting a vegetable garden, or painting the house, consider making it a family affair with everyone having an assigned task. This practice can help build family cohesion and a sense of identity. Be sure to give clear instructions. Tell the child, "If something I said was unclear, be sure and ask again rather than waste your time and effort." This lets your child know that you value his time and effort and expect him to accept some of the responsibility for the success of the project.

Sometimes there may be unexpected and unplanned chores that the child could be assigned, such as picking up a loaf of bread at the store, searching for your lost cat in the neighborhood, changing the bag and filter on the vacuum cleaner, or doing small repairs around the house. Some parents have everyone in the house take a turn at one of the unexpected chores. Circulate a red laminated card with the word "chore" written on it. The card is given to the next person in line for the next unplanned chore. When the chore comes up, it is his or her turn.

WORKING ON BEHALF OF THE FAMILY

It is fine to have chores that are primarily connected to the child's place in the family, such as cleaning their bedrooms, making their beds, taking care of their pets, and taking care of their things. It is also an excellent idea to have them be solely responsible for chore completion that affects the entire family.

For older children they can make a monthly budget and pay the bills (with you signing the checks), do meal planning and grocery shopping for the week (with receipts), or make all of the medical and dental appointments for family members (written and verified). You can also have simple, routine chores that everyone does together, such as doing the laundry or making dinner: "Okay, we're having tacos tonight. Jenny, you fry the meat, Mark, you shred the veggies, and Dad and I will make the salsa and drinks and set the table."

POSITIVE REINFORCEMENT

As for rewards for routine, expected and assigned chores, as someone once said, the only reward the child needs is praise for a job well done; good behavior is its own reward. However, especially with difficult and defiant kids, when you are first attempting to establish a new behavior—such as chore completion—it is an excellent idea to include chores in your point system, or to contract for chore completion (see chapter 5). However, the point system/contract for chores works equally well for kids without any history of defiant behavior. When the behavior is ingrained, you can withdraw the points or the incentives in the contract, and usually the new behavior will stay in place. As adults, we perform our chores because our parents or caregivers taught us to do so, and any incentives we may have gotten at the time are long forgotten.

WORK FOR PAY

If you want to teach your kids the work ethic, then hire them to do jobs around the house or in your business in the same fashion that you would hire any worker. Pay at least the minimum wage (or a set amount for the job). Be sure to specify exactly what is to be done, how it is to be done, and when it is to be done. A good way to do this is with an if/then contract (see chapter 5). This is a business arrangement between you and your child, so feel free to treat it as such. McDonald's has a six-hundred-page operations manual that specifies in the minutest detail how to do every job in the restaurant. Your child should expect no less of a business arrangement from you than he expects from a clown.

Chapter Fifteen

Fighting

Sample consequence rules: Never hit someone else. Never deliberately hurt or injure someone else or take their things. Never destroy property.
Natural consequences: Being feared and disliked by child peers and their parents. The child is socially rejected and isolated. The child is constantly in fights with the risk of injury or retaliation.
Logical consequences: School sanctions for fighting (in-school detention, suspensions, or expulsions). The child is dismissed from community activities (clubs, sports teams, social outings). For older children, legal sanctions—arrest and possible juvenile detention. Loss of privileges and freedom, work details, cleaning the oven, or the garage, scrubbing the toilets, community service, making formal apologies and paying restitution to victims.
Active consequences: Intercession, networking, tracking, monitoring, and supervision.

Children who are frequently involved in fights with other children are anxious children. They are anxious about sharing attention, affection, their friends, their possessions, their toys, or themselves. They tend to think that when other children are receiving these things—or they are asked to share them—they are in danger of losing them for themselves. This makes the child feel frustrated and anxious and they use fighting as a means of defending what they have.

It is easy to frequently see this behavior in toddlers. A little girl doesn't want to share her doll; the little boy doesn't want to share his toy truck. Neither child wants the visiting child to ride their tricycle. A toddler becomes upset when the parent holds the neighbor's baby. He or she doesn't want the stranger child to play in his group. The child is frustrated when his cries of

"No!" or "Give me that!" are ignored, he lashes out with his fists or his feet and someone gets hurt.

If this toddler fighting behavior is ignored or excused by the parent, the older child learns to use fighting as a method of lowering anxiety and feeling frustrated. At least some of the time fighting "works." The child is able to secure his own way and protect what is rightfully his. Fighting becomes a defensive behavior because the world cannot be trusted.

As a therapist, I have treated hundreds of young children who like to fight. In my experience there are six primary reasons children who fight, like to fight.

1. **Boredom:** Some kids feel anxious when they think that there is nothing to do. It is frustrating to be bored. Some bored kids enjoy taunting other children, or provoking them into a verbal altercation or a fist-fight. Fighting stirs things up, it is energizing, and it certainly relieves boredom. Children who fight out of boredom typically are not thinking about the consequences that will result from fighting, and when you ask them why they were fighting they will frequently tell you, "I don't know; I just did," which is a truthful answer. Careful consideration had nothing to do with it.

2. **Habit:** Fighting is an ingrained behavior with some children. It is an old and trusted friend. If a child has repeatedly "won" in a fight with another youngster, the behavior has been strongly reinforced and will re-occur until it is a habitual behavior. It doesn't take long for a behavior to become a habit—in most people it takes about three weeks—and it certainly is true with even very young children. Fighting is very self-reinforcing because you have the opportunity to expend many negative feelings and energy. It is also much more pleasant for some children than having to share, be nice, or be cooperative.

3. **Differences:** Some children have a very difficult time appreciating and accepting differences as they occur with people. Children will "decide" that they don't like an individual or a distinct group of people because they are different. They speak a foreign language, they dress differently, they practice a different religion, and they have different customs and ways of doing things. It doesn't take long for the child to further decide that the person of color, the one who has a handicap, the one who is poor, the one who is rich, the one who is new, and so on, makes the child feel anxious and is not to be trusted. Sometimes, too, this perception is fueled by the prejudice of adults who willingly infect the child with the virus of hatred and intolerance. Children take out their negative feelings by fighting through them. The easiest way is to fight other children who are different.

4. **Resentment:** Children who fight frequently are resentful children. They resent what they do not have that others do have. He has lots of friends. She does well in school, and can spell and do math past her grade level. He has two parents. She gets to go places and have fun. His parents buy him new clothes and he has a cell phone. This sense of frustration and injustice makes resentful children want to bully and fight the child who they perceive to be more fortunate.

5. **Acceptance:** Some children with low self-regard want desperately to be accepted. They want to be liked and appreciated and admired. There is nothing wrong with that. However, some children believe that they will be accepted if they are feared. The best way to instill fear is to be fearsome. Fighting establishes that they are tough and not to be crossed or messed with. Fighting is a handy tool to establish a reputation and to gain acceptance from those who fear you.

6. **Fun:** Fighting is a fun and worthwhile activity for some kids. It feels good to pound somebody. Sometimes too, what starts out as "fun" quickly devolves into fighting. Teasing that turns to hurtful taunts: "You have a face like a monkey"; "Oh no, Loser Johnson is up to bat. There goes the ballgame." Or built-up anger while playing that leads to direct challenges to fight: "You couldn't fight your way out of a paper bag, you wuss. Come on, fight me." Usually, the fun turns serious as a result of arguing and bullying behavior that the child perceives as play. "Hey, I was just kidding. He took it all wrong. I had to defend myself."

All six of the frequent reasons that children like to fight are morally wrong. Continual fighting leaves the child with a skewed sense of how the world works and how to advance in it. Fighting leads to social rejection by the child's peers, alienation from adults, risk of harm, and constant trouble for the child. So how do we stop childhood fighting?

NATURAL AND LOGICAL CONSEQUENCES

For the child who has been in only a few fights, the natural and logical consequences can be of significant help in deterring the child from developing the habit of fighting. The child learns from the consequences that fighting is more troublesome than it is worth. For the child who has been in numerous fights—including verbal altercations, bullying, and fights with siblings as well as peers—the natural and logical consequences are the cost of doing business and often will not have lasting effect in deterring fighting in the future. For these children, use active consequences.

ACTIVE CONSEQUENCES

Intercession

Teach your children that fighting is not just wrong, it is stupid. No one outside a small circle of dunces will think that the child is cool, smart, or tough because they have skill in calling others names, because they can get their way through fear and intimidation, or that assault is productive. Teach your child your moral or religious values about fighting. Teach your children that fighting causes pain and suffering without reason. Teach your children to treat others in the way they themselves wish to be treated. The respect and regard that they want for themselves are what they must give in order to get. Name calling, threatening, or beating up someone who is weaker are the hallmarks of a coward. It takes someone with skill and courage to respect the differences, the rights, and feelings of others.

Networking

Ask your personal network for information about your child's fighting behavior. If they see it or hear of it, ask them to contact you immediately. There is a reason frequent fighters like to "schedule" a fight away from the school grounds, the playground, out in the woods, or some other hidden place. They don't want to be seen. Networking with as many adults as you can will give you the advantage because the child never knows when a trusted adult may be watching, and networking acts as an alert as well as a deterrent.

Tracking

Look for the signs, the physical evidence that the child has been fighting. Torn clothes, cuts and scratches, scuffed knuckles, or the child having unexplained items that they did not have before—toys, electronic gadgets, money, jewelry, backpacks, food, and the like that may have been stolen from fight victims.

Monitoring

Children who fight habitually cannot do so successfully when they are being monitored consistently. Know the basics: where the child is, who they are with, and what they are doing. Repeat the consequence rule often. Target fighting behavior in your monitoring anytime and anywhere in your home; tell the child that before he goes to the park, playground, to the friend's house, to the mall, the movies, the arcade, the pool, or other places that they like to frequent, that you and other trusted adults are *listening* and *watching* for rude remarks or gestures, for threatening behavior, or for physical fighting behavior for *any* reason. The first time it happens, the child will immediately be removed and taken home.

Supervision

Supervision is a more stringent form of monitoring. The child has little to no free time for a set period so they have limited to no opportunity to engage in fighting. This means that for a time, the child has no unsupervised time; they are under the eyeball supervision of a trusted adult.

Another good method to ensure supervision is successful is to use the six-day level system as an alternative to grounding and taking away privileges. You can also use grounding for a few days and then give the child a small amount of freedom with peer social interactions. "Anthony, you can have a half-hour of play time with your friends today. If you handle that well without fighting, you can have a half-hour tomorrow. Then an hour of play time, and then more time until you can have all of the time you wish before you need to do something else. But if there is any fighting, you will immediately come back into the house for the rest of the day, and can try again the next day."

PRAISE AND REWARDS

Consistently praise the child for choosing to not fight. "Gabby, you did a wonderful thing today at day care. You didn't hit any of the other children." "Sammy, I am so proud of you for not name calling and for sharing your toys this afternoon." This kind of recognition for positive behavior is exactly the sort of attention that many children who fight crave to hear and to have. The same is true when you use rewards for the positive opposite behavior of not fighting. You can also use a behavior contract or the point system to reward the targeted behavior of not fighting.

Fighting behavior with children will cease if you make it so. When children do not use their hands for hurting, and use their hearts for sharing, they gain a whole new perspective on the world and their rightful place in it. What a wonderful outcome.

Chapter Sixteen

Friends

Sample consequence rules: Bring all of your friends to the house so that I can meet them. Bring all of the friends you wish to associate with to the house so I can meet them. Always ask permission if you wish to do something with _____ . Never associate with _____ .
Natural consequence: The child has experiences with his/her friends.
Logical consequences: Parent restricts or increases contact with the friend based upon child's behavior choices.
Active consequences: Intercession, networking, tracking, monitoring, and supervision.

Young children have a different way of making friends than do older ones. From about the age of three to seven most children have friendships based upon the other child's willingness to play and play cooperatively. Friendships at this age are generally not much of an issue for parents.

Friendships become more involved when children become a little older. And that is when parents may become involved or concerned about the child's choice of friends. Conflict can follow.

The most common rallying cry of childhood is, "You can't choose my friends!" That's right, you can't. You can certainly influence and guide your child in the choice of friends, but the ultimate choice is the child's. Likewise, the behavior choices the child makes while with his friends are his. So are all the resulting consequences. So should we permit our child to experience whatever may come when with the friend? To a certain extent, yes. Our children need these experiences to understand the intricacies of personal relationships. They will discover for themselves whom they trust and can count on, and whom they must steer clear of. For most children, next to their

parents and loved ones, their friends are the single most important and in-
fluential people in their lives. We should hope they choose them with care.

KNOW THE FRIENDS

What do you do if you're concerned about your child getting into trouble
when with his friend? First, start with a reality check. Establish a consequence rule about the need to meet all of your child's friends. (If you can
meet the child's parents at the same time, so much the better.) Have your
child write down the name, address, and phone number of each of his friends
in an address book. He can do this every time he makes a new friend. Carry a
list of friends' names, home and email addresses, and phone numbers with
you at all times; some parents put the list in their personal electronic devices.

NETWORKING

You want to get to know your child's friends—and their parents. Ask them
over for dinner or coffee, or meet them at the soccer game, the park, or the
mall. But make it a point to meet them. Ask polite and friendly questions.
Later, suggest that the kids spend some time at your house. Try to get a sense
of what the friends' values are and what they think is important. If they
appear to be good kids with good families, you're done. If a red flag goes up
in your head, tell your child your concerns. If he wants to continue to see the
kid, tell him that you shall hold him personally accountable for all of his
behavior choices when he is with the friend. If he makes appropriate choices,
how long he sees the friend is up to him. If not, then restrict him from seeing
the friend. The more serious the behavior problems, the more serious you'll
be about restricting access.

In a very few cases, there may be no access. None. Zip. Zero. These are
kids who are enmeshed in crime and violence and who wish to recruit your
child's participation. How do you stop your child's contact with these kids?

MONITORING

Many of these older kids—age ten and up—are wards of the juvenile court
and are on probation. In most states you have the right to find out if a child of
concern is a ward of the court. If so, request that the court officer inform this
child that he or she is not to associate with your child by making this a
condition of the probation (if your child is on probation then it's even easier).
If he continues to do so, he will be violating the court's order. The last thing a
child in the juvenile justice system wants is to be back in court over a matter
as seemingly minor as being friends with your kid. There is always some

other kid whose parents do not monitor his friendships that he can hook up with.

Well, won't some children likely sneak around to still see each other? Probably. And won't some kids just flat defy their parent's attempts to restrict access? Could be. And didn't I say earlier that would just make the other kid appear to be more attractive in the eyes of your child? I did.

The key is to restrict access on the *parent's* terms. The kids can still talk on the phone, text, send email, see each other at school, and be at the house together, but because they shoplifted at the store, they can't go shopping together. Because they got into trouble when together, your child and his friend can go to the movies together, the football game together, and skateboarding, but only under a parent or trusted adult's direct supervision for a specified number of days. And your son and his friends are not to be in the house together without a chaperone because they were caught playing prohibited video games.

INTERCESSION

What if the problem behavior is more serious or continuous? Then your consequences need to be more serious and continuous. Start with intercession. Communicate your specific concerns about the friend using Straight Talk. If you have a loving relationship with your child, it will greatly increase your chances of being heard and heeded.

An easy way to formalize the process is to place your child's friends in mental categories. An *A* category child is a child that you know, a child whose parents you know and trust. Your child can do anything within reason when with this friend without your needing to be concerned or involved. This should be the majority of all the friends your child is involved with.

The *B* category kid is one that you don't know. Depending upon how trustworthy your child has been in the past when he has been with friends, you *may* need to restrict access on your terms, or until the two kids have a history of satisfactory behavior choices when together.

A *C* category child is one who has a history of unacceptable behavior when he has been with your child. When the two kids are together, they require monitoring and supervision, or no contact for a specified period of time.

Finally, a *D* category friend is one that has a criminal, violent, and/or substance abuse history and is seeking to recruit your child into the same activity. This friend is not to associate with your child. Period. You enforce this restriction by any legal means necessary.

Can kids move from one category to another? Sure they can. It all depends upon what your child chooses to do when she is with her friend.

Further, if an *A* category child engages in some serious misbehavior when with your child, he or she can move to the *C* category for thirty days, or, alternatively, you can have a no contact period for thirty days.

A word of caution. If you say something like "I know he's involved in using drugs. He's got a Mohawk and a nose ring," you'll sound ridiculous to your child. Because the kid listens to punk bands, dresses all in black, or has a foul mouth is not a sure sign of anything, including that your child will follow suit.

NEED FOR BELONGING

If your child does follow along, it most likely means he or she tends to be easily influenced and is hungry for emotional attachments. If your child becomes involved in criminal or harmful antisocial activity when with the friend, be ready and be armed. Be ready to restrict and in some cases completely stop contact with the negative friend. Be armed with the *facts* of what you know about the friend's behavior and your child's behavior when with the friend.

Sometimes your child's situation is compounded by entanglement with a negative friend who abuses them or takes advantage of them. "You don't understand, Dad. He didn't mean to do that. He is not like that; he really is a nice person." Here your child is wading out into swift currents and doesn't even know he is getting wet. In addition to restriction, you should seek professional therapeutic help for the child who is abused or who is emotionally attached to antisocial friends and can't seem to stop the association. There are better ways to belong.

MONITORING AND NETWORKING

What about the child who has "secret" friends—friends whom your child never brings to the house and doesn't want you to meet? Here you must carefully and consistently monitor *where* your child goes, *whom* he says he is with, and *what* he says they are doing. If there is wrongdoing, the secret friend will eventually turn up. If there is no wrongdoing, then your child should have no qualms about introducing his friend. Stipulate you will turn down the heat on monitoring their activities when you meet "all" of his friends.

Also, you can ask your network for help. Some people may be able to tell you whom your child is hanging out with and what their names and reputation might be. "Well, I don't know if they're friends, but I've seen her hanging out with so and so and this person's reputation is thus and so."

FURTHER INTERCESSION

Some kids have difficulty making and sustaining friendships. There are very specific things kids can do to make friends, and to avoid getting into trouble when with certain friends. Have your child talk to the school counselor or a family therapist to learn these skills. Also, encourage your child to move in circles where he is more likely to meet kids with positive attitudes and values—places of worship, volunteer groups, youth camps, activity clubs, sports teams, and the like.

Some children are so unsure of themselves and their lives that they gravitate toward peer groups that seemingly have the answers. Kids who habitually lie, steal, cheat, assault others, and dabble in other antisocial activity no more have the right plans for your child than the serpent did for Eve. Groups of these children have an almost magnetic attraction for some kids because they can provide many of the same supportive characteristics as traditional families.

PEER INFLUENCE

A large body of research shows that children vary widely in the extent to which their peers influence their behavior. Studies demonstrate conclusively that children are much more likely to be heavily influenced when the quality of the parent-child relationship is poor, when self-regard is low, when they believe they are frequently criticized and emotionally rejected, and when they believe communication is spotty with little encouragement for positive behavior.

Further, kids who have immature, impulsive, narcissistic, and emotionally unattached personalities are especially likely to be influenced by negative peers and groups. But even these kids don't *run* into delinquency and other problems, they *drift* into them.

Children want desperately to fit in and to be accepted by their peers. There is nothing wrong with that. The experience your child has in making and sustaining friendships is the anvil on which adult relationships are hammered out. As parents, we want to be sure that our children can complete the work successfully.

Chapter Seventeen

Information Technology

Sample consequence rules: Follow all the rules for using the computer. They are listed under the file name "rules." Never post identifying information about yourself to strangers. Always guard your password. Always ask permission if you are not sure what to do.
Natural consequence: The child will have experiences of different kinds on the computer.
Logical consequences: Time restrictions on computer use. Filtering and parental control devices in place.
Active consequences: Intercession, networking, tracking, monitoring, and supervision.

My fourteen-year-old daughter knows more about using her computer than I do mine. In the twenty first century, children's lives will be evermore intertwined with their personal computer, especially with the Internet. Rather than going off to search the world, the Internet brings the world to them. There are many wonderful things on the Internet for kids to learn, see, and do. Unfortunately, the Internet also has nests of vipers that parents must guard against. They crawl into our homes through the portal of cyberspace.

If your child surfs the Internet, makes social contacts, and uses the computer in responsible and trustworthy ways consistently, then let them continue to do so. You only need to establish some reasonable guidelines and rules.

RESTRICT PERSONAL INFORMATION

Think about the social networking sites your child may be involved with. Most kids post personal profiles, photographs, messages, and even names, addresses, and phone numbers for the entire world to see to attract attention and new friends—often without their parent's knowledge. Revealing too much personal information not only is incredibly dangerous, but can also be perused at some point by prospective employers, college admissions boards, and criminals for years to come. If your child has or is involved in social network websites, you'll need to establish rules for its use.

DEALING WITH EXPLOITATION

Think about the people your child will come into contact with while online. Consider using the same mental categories for people your child has contact with on the Internet that you have in the three-dimensional world:

- An *A* category: A person you know and trust.
- A *B* category: A person you don't know.
- A *C* category: A person who has gotten into trouble with your child through computer contacts.
- A *D* category: A person who has solicited or engaged in criminal behavior with your child as a result of computer contacts.

An *A* category person may have unsupervised contact with your child. A *B* category person you need more information about. A *C* category person has no computer contact with your child for thirty days, or your child has a thirty-day computer restriction. A *D* category person has no contact whatsoever with your child, and you file a police report about the wrongdoing.

The Department of Justice reports that one in five children is known to have received adult sexual solicitations online. Most of these adults lie about who they are, their age, and what they want from the child, although many pedophiles are brazen about stating their age and intention. Have a rule that you are to be told immediately if anyone asks personal information or for a meeting—regardless of how old that person claims to be, or benign their stated intentions.

If your child is in the habit of posting inappropriate content on his or her webpage, or accepts solicitations from strangers, tell your child he or she must post a prominently displayed statement on the webpage that says, in essence, "I am twelve years old and this is a monitored website."

TRACKING

When exploiters or predators see such a message, they will move on to hunt for easier prey. If your child refuses to post the message, block all access to the computer until they do. Then go online periodically to check the website for content and the posted message. Also, periodically scan the Internet for images and information about your child that may have been downloaded by others for their own purposes. If you need to play it safe, then do so. Educate your child about the dangers of the Internet. Install and use filtering and parental control devices. Block everything that is not pre-approved or is not under the heading of approved guidelines. Limit engagement with chat rooms to those that are monitored, or ones that contain safe topics. Locate the computer in a family area of your home where you can supervise its use. Network with the school, the public library, and your child's friends' parents about computer use in their location or home.

If your child has a cell phone, tablet, or other electronic device, understand its capability to download images and software and to receive and send text messages. Use the same safety measures with the device that you have in place for the computer. Some cell phone companies set limits on minutes and messages, send family priority messages, and control the time of day and day of the week the phone can be used. These steps will not ensure your child's safe journey in cyberspace, but they will make it much more likely that your child will not drive off a cliff.

PREVENTATIVE SUPERVISION

Finally, if (or when) your child is trustworthy with computer use, establish a twenty-four-hour rule. Tell your child that you trust that he or she is making good decisions when online (the vast majority of kids do) *and* you will continue to monitor the computer. This is what you can say:

1. I respect your privacy.
2. In twenty-four hours I will go online to your website or blog to check for content.
3. You have twenty-four hours to remove anything that is inappropriate or store anything that you do not wish me to see or to read.

Information technology is here to stay. Like fire, it is a wondrous tool that has transformed the human condition. And like our ancestors, we want to make sure that our children do not fall into the fire pit.

Chapter Eighteen

Lying

Sample consequence rules: Never lie. Always tell the truth. Always tell me the whole truth when I ask you about something.
Natural consequences: People do not believe what the child says. People question what he/she says. People do not trust him/her. Child has a reputation as a liar.
Logical consequences: Every time the child lies, he/she needs to make restitution by apology, payment, or service.
Active consequences: Networking, intercession.

All children lie at some time. Sometimes the lie is not intentional but is based on fantasy, "We went to Mars and I found $50 under a pile of rocks." Later on, around the age of four children learn to lie to try to avoid embarrassment or punishment. And sometimes, just like adults, kids lie to gain something they want. When an older child lies, he typically lies for the same reasons. Usually, however, he is more adept at lying than is a young child because he has more experience. And, of course, some older kids never lie.

NATURAL AND LOGICAL CONSEQUENCES

If a child lies rarely or infrequently, which is the case with most kids, it is best to let the child experience the natural consequence of lying or the lie. The essence of the logical consequence for lying is to make restitution. The child needs to make formal apologies to the person or place that was lied to. Or he needs to make payment by losing a privilege that is logically related to the lie. For example, your child lied about his whereabouts—he said he was going over to Bob's house to play, but he went to the park to meet Sally—he should be restricted from going out for a few days, and in having contact with

Sally. As a result of his lying, he will now have the experience of losing your trust for a while. He can try again in a few days to begin earning trust once again.

NETWORKING

If a child is lying frequently, use the active consequence consistently. The art of lying has practical value to the child only when he can pass the lie. If he knows that you will verify every lie, or potential lie, lying will quickly lose its practical value and effectiveness. Ask the network to contact you if anyone thinks your child is lying. Your child will quickly learn that lying is counterproductive and can lead to the very embarrassment and consequences that he was trying to avoid by lying in the first place.

TRUTH-TELLING

Further, you can greatly increase your odds of the child giving up lying by doing two things. The first is to praise your child consistently when you have certain knowledge that they are telling you the truth when you have asked them about something. Second, use the point system (chapter 5) to target lying as a behavior you want to see less of, and truth telling as a behavior you want to see more of.

GOING TO THE SOURCE

Even when they know the truth, some parents like to question their child in hopes of "catching" them in the act of lying. It is pointless to ask the kid with orange teeth if they ate all of the Cheetos. This practice usually only encourages children to continue to lie in order to support the first lie. If you're not sure this is a lie, check it out every time. You do this by *going to the source*. Check directly with the teacher, the neighbor, the friend's parents, and so on to get their version of what transpired.

TRAINING A CHILD NOT TO LIE

You can also directly train your child not to lie. Give the child with a history of lying a chance to clarify seemingly conflicting facts or statements by using the "you said A, she said B," procedure: "Your teacher said that she counted you absent, that you did not come in late. You said that you got to class after attendance was taken. Now before I impose a consequence for lying, which one of you is correct or did I misunderstand what you said?"

A second training method is to tell your child, "This is the truth as I know it to be": "Doug, this is the truth as I know it to be. I know you didn't go to your Aunt Edna's today. What I don't know is where you went when you finished school. Now before you have a consequence for lying, would you care to tell me where you were?"

Give your child the chance to back out of the lie, before a double consequence is imposed (one for lying, one for the misbehavior), and he can still save face. Like politicians who are caught in a lie, they didn't really "lie"—they "misspoke." Fine, let's have the truth now.

If you're not sure of the truth you can say, "I will check it out; my information is different." Then go back to the source and check it out. If you have suspicion, but no evidence of wrongdoing, you can say "I believe" followed by an inquiry: "I believe that my tools have been used. Do you know anything about that?" "I believe that some of the cookies I baked for the party have been eaten. What can you tell me about that?"

INTERCESSION

If a child is lying habitually, it usually means something else is going on besides lying. She is engaging in a variety of undesirable or forbidden behaviors that she wants to cover up, or there is an emotional problem that needs to be addressed in counseling. Either way, be ready to intercede with available help

Chapter Nineteen

Manners

Sample consequence rules: Always treat others with kindness and respect. Always use the "magic words": please, thank you, excuse me, and I'm sorry. Always ask me, or another trusted adult, if you are unsure what is the polite thing to do.

Natural consequences: The child has a reputation as being ill-mannered and impolite. The child is avoided or socially rejected by other children or adults.

Logical consequences: Overcorrection; response cost; or is placed in time-out for ill-mannered behavior.

Active consequences: Intercession, monitoring, and networking.

There is nothing quite as pleasant as the well-mannered child. There is nothing quite as unpleasant as the ill-mannered child. No one—child or adult—enjoys being around a child who is rude, obnoxious, and self-centered. It is not enough to expect children to learn the social graces by observing others; they must be taught them by their parents and other caregivers. The good news is that this is an easy thing to do.

You can begin teaching children manners as early as when they are two years old, but certainly no later than by the time they are three years old. Here is a list of common manners that children should know and be practicing by the time they are eight years old. This is a manners list that my wife and I constructed for our daughter when she was little:

1. When asking for or receiving something, say "please" and "thank you."
2. Say "excuse me" and "I'm sorry" when necessary.
3. Unless it is an emergency, do not interrupt when someone is speaking or in a conversation.

4. Do not point at or whisper about others.
5. When you are in doubt about doing something, always ask permission.
6. Do not comment on people's looks, unless it is to compliment them.
7. Knock on closed doors and then wait for a response before entering.
8. When you speak on the home phone, always say hello, and then say your first name.
9. Sit quietly, even when you are bored.
10. Never call people names.
11. Never make fun of anyone for any reason.
12. Never start an argument or a fight.
13. Always observe table manners when eating.
14. Always acknowledge a gift or an act of kindness with a thank you.
15. Always use good words when you are upset or angry, and never shout, swear, or hit.

Now, you can certainly make your own list. You may have certain expected manners for your children that are important to you. It is a family value with some parents that children address adults as "Sir" or "Ma'am"; that adults be addressed by only their last names with a Mr., Mrs., or Ms.; that children not run in crowds or onto elevators; that children greet everyone they encounter at religious services; that children be especially polite to their teachers and the elderly—and so on. When you make your list, choose the manners that you think are important for your child to practice or that you especially want to work on establishing with your child.

MANNERS AND RESPECT

A wise saying is "Respect is what you have to give in order to receive." Manners and respect are inseparable. You cannot have one without the other. Respect means treating others with kindness and consideration. Children first learn respect by having it displayed to them by their parents. I have regretted the disrespectful and ill-mannered behavior that I have displayed to my daughter over the years. I've had to review the fifteen-item manners list many times to see where I could do better and to make a commitment to doing so. And I believe that partly because of that my fourteen-year-old daughter is very respectful to everyone, including her parents. The same can be true for you.

THE GOLDEN RULE OF PARENTING

Someone coined The Golden Rule of Parenting: "Always be the person you want your child to be." As difficult as this sounds it really means being a positive role model for your child. I want my child or children to work on one or more of the behaviors on the manners list. Do I model the desired behavior? I am already in the habit of saying "please," "thank you," "excuse me" and "I'm sorry" when necessary because *my* parents taught *me* to do so. But what do I role model for my child when I do not sit quietly when I'm bored? Or when I call people names? Or when I start an argument? Certainly I am modeling an ill-mannered behavior that my child will realize I do not really think is important to avoid and that she will likely imitate.

So I always need from an early age not only to say "please" and "thank you" to the child for what they have done that is pleasing, but I must also work on consistently role modeling all of the items on the manners list. By doing so not only will my child imitate the positive behaviors, but imitate avoiding the negative ones as well.

INTERCESSION: FIVE STEPS TO TEACH MANNERS

Here are five intercession steps that you can do that will greatly increase the chances of your child learning and observing manners.

1. **Work on targeted manner behaviors:** From your manners list identify one or two behaviors that you want to work on establishing with your child. For very young children you may start with the basics of saying "please," and "thank you." For older children it may be table manners and saying "I'm sorry" when necessary. For older children still target problem manner behavior that may be occurring such as running into crowds, waiting for the elevator to empty, not interrupting, and asking permission. As the child approaches five or six, they should be well on the way to observing most of the manner behaviors listed, and by age eight they should have the list mastered.
2. **Be tolerant of manner mistakes, but do not overlook them:** Do not yell at or frighten the child when they fail to perform a certain manner behavior that you are working on together. Correct them by saying what they could have done better or differently. "Ray, we always greet people by saying 'good morning' when we first enter the church."
3. **Give a prompt:** Give children a chance to correct their own manner behavior with a gentle reminder. "Suzie, did you ask permission before looking in Grandma's refrigerator?"
4. **Praise your child:** We have discussed the importance of praise to increase the chances of the child engaging in a positive behavior that we want to see repeated. This is certainly true when teaching manners. Remember to praise the child in public for all to hear, and offer constructive criticism in private for only one to hear. "Ray, I am so

pleased that you greeted everyone you met in church today. That was
super!" "Suzie, I noticed that you asked Grandma for permission before looking in her refrigerator. That was very polite."

5. **Reward your child:** When you are first attempting to establish manner behavior, you may want to offer the child a small positive incentive for observing the manner behavior. Remember, you can fade the
rewards once the new positive behavior is in place. "Ray and Suzie,
you followed the table manners at the restaurant and you didn't get
into an argument or a fight. Let's stop for ice cream as we agreed."

DISCIPLINE METHODS

A few children are actively resistant to using manners, or need mild discipline to ensure that they follow through on observing manners in the future.
Here are some methods that may be useful.

- **Overcorrection:** Have the child repeat the correct mannered behavior
several times in a row. "Go back and walk through the door, but this time
see if you can hold the door open for someone coming after you." "Next
time do not reach for food across the table, ask to have the food passed,
and say 'thank you.' Let's practice."
- **Response Cost:** "Because you refused to let the younger kids have a turn,
go to the time out chair." "Because you threw food at each other, you and
your brother will clean the dining room and have an extra turn in doing the
dishes."
- **Monitoring:** "There have been problems with using manners you've
learned at other people's homes. Today I'll be monitoring what you
choose to do while we are visiting."
- **Networking:** "Hello Mrs. Johnson. I am working with Jamie about taking
turns on the playground. I'd like to request that the playground monitor
call me after recess if Jamie does not let other children have a turn on the
swing. Thank you."

Teaching children manners will pay them dividends their entire lives.
Permitting children to be ill-mannered will do them a disservice their entire
lives. People respect, admire, and appreciate children who are well-mannered. The opposite is also true. Do reinforce these behaviors and you will
have a polite, thoughtful, and well-liked child that you will be proud to take
anywhere.

Chapter Twenty

School Assignments and Homework

Sample consequence rules: Complete all of your assignments before they are due. Turn in all of your completed assignments when they are due. Complete all of your homework every night it is assigned. Complete all of your school projects before they are due.

Natural consequences: Child fails the subject or the grade.

Logical consequences: Child studies at home for a set period of time until the teacher verifies that he/she is completely caught up.

Active consequences: Tracking, monitoring, supervision, networking, and intercession.

Most children want to be successful in school. Children spend so much of their lives in school that they want to be able to feel that it is a good place to be. As parents, we want them to feel that way about school as well.

Children who do not do well in school usually start going off track in the late elementary grades or junior high school. This is often when parents start losing track of what is happening with the child in school. It is often not that the parent doesn't care; it's just that the child now has more difficult work to do, may have multiple teachers, and doesn't talk about school as much as he used to.

Some kids become distracted by personal issues, family problems, or the influence of negative peers. Still others at middle school age get drawn into truancy, delinquency, substance abuse, or antisocial activities that take them away from school. Some parents believe it's the school's responsibility to educate the child and that they are just doing a "lousy" job of it. Perhaps so. Regardless if the child is enrolled in a "lousy" school or not, you can help your child be consistently successful in school.

NATURAL CONSEQUENCES

Some parent educators and some teachers believe kids should be allowed to experience the natural consequences of failing the subject or the grade. Children should have the "freedom to fail" because they'll learn to do better next time. This belief puts the child at risk for harm and is ill conceived. The freedom to fail philosophy teaches a child only one thing: how to fail. We want to teach our children how to succeed.

LOGICAL CONSEQUENCES

Using a logical consequence is more productive. When you see the progress report or report card that shows your child failing one or more subjects, you know that he is having difficulty not only in class, but also in completing homework.

Help or direct your child to set up a study time and place at home to complete daily assignments, homework, and longer-term projects. Make sure this is a place with plenty of space, light, and quiet. The kitchen or dining room table may be an ideal location after meal preparation and eating are over. To begin with it is usually best to have the child devote a small amount of time to schoolwork. Help your child be consistently successful with fifteen or twenty minutes of study time a day and then within two weeks increase the time to a half hour, then forty-five minutes, an hour, and then as much time as is needed (the time begins *after* she has returned from the bathroom and sharpened all of her pencils). If she has more schoolwork than can be completed in fifteen minutes, have her work in fifteen-minute increments with a five-minute break. In two weeks, increase the time to a half hour, then forty-five minutes, an hour, and then as much time as is needed.

ACTIVE CONSEQUENCES

Intercession

If you only know that the child is failing one or more subjects or classes but you don't know why, intercede by pinpointing the reasons. Is he not paying attention in class? Goofing off in class? Not even in class? Is he not turning in the assigned work, failing exams, or not participating in class? Is it that he seemingly cannot do the work? Certainly you want to network with his teachers and school counselor, but you can also find out a good deal of what you need to know to answer these questions by using the School Behavior Checklist provided on the website.

If he seems to struggle with the subject, assist your child with tutoring and guidance. Check to see if his school offers tutoring help before, during, or after the school day. There are also a number of reputable tutoring business services and some available online. Also, many schools have adult mentors who can be a source of great help. Find out what your child's school has to offer.

For kids who are actively resisting doing even a short period of schoolwork, hire a "friendly gorilla" to sit with them and to help them get started. Review their assignments with them before they turn them in to the teacher. When homework is completed, have the child lay out their clothes and supplies and ready their backpack the *night before* the next day. This practice helps the child be mentally prepared for the next school day.

Tracking and Networking

If these interventions are not helping to raise your child's grades, consider using a Daily Class Assignment Report which each teacher signs to indicate that your child attended classes, behaved appropriately, completed classwork, and turned in homework, until grades improve. Your child needs to bring the report home each day with the signature of each teacher (if they have more than one). This strategy strengthens the network and the connection with the school as a whole. Some parents will need a "signature list" of all of the teachers, just to be sure that their child isn't engaging in a little creative writing: "Sorry son, no sale; this doesn't even look close to Mr. Johnson's signature." You can also do random phone checks about the assignments and in many cases communicate with teachers through email and fax. If you think your child may intercept written messages or grade reports, have these sent to the neighbor's house or to a post office box. Ask teachers and others to report to you any improvements that your child is making. This process will encourage teachers to praise your child, which in turn will up the odds for continued improvement.

If your child balks at the idea of carrying the Daily Class Assignment Report, give him the option of your going to school with him a half hour before school starts and talking to each of his teachers. Tell him that you will be happy to do this every time you need to in order to know how he is doing in class. Suddenly, carrying the assignment report won't look so bad.

If your child "forgets" to bring home the Daily Class Assignment Report, or has left it on the bus, in her locker, at Ted's house, and so on, accompany her while she retrieves it. Some parents have the school fax them the daily report. If the reason is "the teacher wouldn't sign it," go with your kid the next school day and talk to the teacher and request that they sign it. Have the child carry the daily report until grades and behavior improve, then a weekly report, and finally a monthly report. When all is as it should be, throw the assignment sheets away.

Yeah, but what if one or more of the kid's teachers won't cooperate? Then talk to the principal. The easiest way for the principal to handle the situation is to direct the teacher to take ten seconds of her time to review and sign the form. No luck with the principal? Talk to the superintendent, the school board, and on up the chain of command until someone realizes you mean business and resolves the issue in your favor. Extending the concept of the Daily Class Assignment Report, many elementary and secondary schools now have websites that record your child's school assignments and completed work. Your child's record can be accessed via a personal code and is updated daily, so that you can use the DCAR and the website in tandem.

More Intercession

Active intercession can also be useful in more ways as well. In addition to tutoring help, consider enrolling the child in reading dynamic, study skills, computer literacy, and memory improvement classes and workshops—this is also excellent preparation for high school. In addition, there are many useful videos and computer programs that teach math and reading skills, as well as those that teach science, social studies, art, music, and other subjects (see the Internet for more). Some kids have great success organizing and tracking their schoolwork with a PDA (personal data assistant), a thumb drive, or other electronic device. Make a point of seeking out teachers for your child who demand excellence, especially in such critical areas as math and language arts.

On days when your child does not have any homework, you may want to have them stay in the homework routine. Have him or her do a half hour of reading of good literature of their choice (not a paperback with a bronzed hunk or naked nymphs on the cover), or a half hour of learning a new skill on the computer (not a game), or fifteen minutes solving a math puzzle (at their level). Anything that will exercise the brain muscle in a positive way is useful.

Networking

If the teachers think your child may have a learning disability, have him tested. The child may also be tested to find out what his predominant learning style may be. Some kids are primarily visual learners, some are auditory learners, and some are tactile learners, meaning the child may learn best by seeing, hearing, or touching learning material. Learning that takes place in the child's dominant style can be much easier and more productive. Some kids, too, may have attention deficit or attention deficit/hyperactivity disorder, or another biologically-based disorder that has not been detected and may need to be accessed.

Extracurricular Activities

Encourage your child to become active in school-related activities, such as sports teams, drama, band or orchestra, choir, clubs, volunteer activities, student newspaper or yearbook, or student government. Some kids do better in school with an after-school job, such as an afternoon paper route or watering the neighbor's plants. If keeping the job is made a condition of maintaining success in school the job can be a motivator to maintain passing grades and regular attendance.

The reason for your encouragement is because one or more of these positive activities will increase your child's attachments to the school. Children who have such attachments usually do better academically, have higher self-regard, and have fewer behavior problems while at school.

Alternative Sources of Education

If your child struggles with "traditional" schooling, or is behind in middle school credits, inquire if your child's school offers viable alternatives for earning credit: alternative school, online school, summer school, charter school, tutoring classes, public television courses, and courses offered through the Internet. Nowadays anyone who wants an education can get one. Ignorance is not bliss—it's only ignorance.

Reinforcers for Success

Finally, offer frequent praise, acknowledgment, rewards, and encouragement for your child's effort and successes (see chapter 8). Use of the point system and contracting are two excellent ways to encourage school success. The child will do better next semester *and* the next day. Every child can be successful in school. As parents, we can help them build ladders to reach for the stars.

Chapter Twenty-One

Sibling Fighting

Sample consequence rules: Never put each other down. Never say or do anything to be deliberately unkind or to hurt one another. Always seek to settle your differences between yourselves before involving one of your parents.
Natural consequence: Parent "divorces" him/herself from children's sibling conflicts.
Logical consequences: Parent applies conflict resolution and problem-solving skills. Separation, work details, confiscation, forfeiture.
Active consequence: Intervention.

Sibling conflicts are perfectly normal and to be expected. As children get older, sibling conflicts should decrease. If the child is still squabbling frequently with his brother or sister, you should intervene. Intervening can range from refusing to intercede to settling disputes to everyone's satisfaction.

When children get into a scrap about something, they often seek to involve the parent. How often have you heard the earsplitting call of "Mom!!!!" or "Dad!!!!!" when an argument or tussle is going on between your kids? Each wants you to use your authority on his or her behalf. Your kids are not asking you to walk into a dispute and, using your Solomon-like wisdom, render a just and reasonable solution. No, they want you to hammer the other kid. Each kid is betting that you will err on the side of justice and be on his or her side.

What would happen if you removed that parental power leverage? Why, our kids would be forced to resolve their own problems. What a concept!

When your child becomes an adult, who will mediate her disputes with the neighbor? With the boss or the coworker? With her spouse? Does she

171

expect you to jump in the car and go right over to fix everything for her? Not hardly, as the kids would say. Would you want to? Not hardly. Therefore teaching children how to settle their disputes with their siblings should provide good practice for when they have disputes with other adults later on. Still, you could choose to jump in with both feet to resolve your child's disputes for them, unless you have a more pleasant activity planned—such as a root canal—but you would be handicapping your children into thinking that might equals right.

SIBLING FIGHTING

Brothers and sisters often fight about peculiar things.
"Now . . . I told you to quit breathing my air. Now I'm mad."
"Mom! Mom! He just snapped my bra and told me to go bite a mailman."
"You're stupid."
"Oh, yeah? You're more stupid."
"Well, you're stupid and none of my friends like you."
"That's because all your friends are stupid."
"Dad! Dad! He's calling me names."
"Am not! Dad, I didn't say anything, and she started it."
"You can't sit there. I need that chair for my books."
"Bolivia exports tin."
"It does not!"
"Fraid so!"
"Fraid not!"
"Mom, Bolivia exports tin, doesn't it?"
And so on. These kinds of disputes are engaged in mainly for their entertainment value. When such hassles develop between kids, it is generally best not to get involved. Do you really care if Bolivia exports tin? Neither do your kids. The argument is simply jockeying for position, in this case which child knows the most about Bolivia.

Sometimes too siblings fight each other about things as well as ideas: who can use the computer, wear each other's clothes, be in the other's bedroom, what TV show or movie to watch. But do you really want to mediate a war for the umpteenth time over whether they can watch a rerun of *Star Trek* or cartoon shows on a cable channel?

INTERCESSION AND CONSEQUENCES

When the bickering starts to escalate into loud voices and putdowns, parents should intercede. (If one kid is soaking the other kid's head in a bucket of ice water, go ahead and intercede here too.) Restate the consequence rules about sibling fighting. Resist the temptation to get into a referee, prosecutor, defense attorney, or judge's role. Tell the siblings to immediately stop the quarreling and to not start again—ever. If the quarrel does start up again, *immediately* impose a logical or active consequence. Don't threaten, just do it. For example, if they can't be in the same room together peacefully, should they be in the same room? No. Send one to the bathroom and one to the garage. If they need something to do while they are marooned there, have them clean it (some parents have exceptionally clean bathrooms and garages). If you're in the car, pull over to the side of the road until things calm down (although this intervention works better if you're driving to Disneyland rather than the dentist). Here the consequence (such as the work detail) comes about when you return home. The same is true when you are out in the community somewhere; alternatively, whether in or out of the house and the kids start a ruckus, use confiscation or forfeiture.

If they are in the house, when the can they come out of time-out/isolation and be together again? When they can do so peacefully. But how will you know that they can?

PROBLEM SOLVING

Teach brothers and sisters exactly how to resolve conflicts and actively solve problems by teaching the skills in chapter 8, "Conflict Resolution with Children." This intervention works well because when people are forced to find a solution to a common problem, they tend to find common ground. As a result they learn to see their sibling not as an enemy but as an ally.

When a brawl starts, interrupt and immediately have the kids begin using the skills. Tell them you'll be waiting for their decision, and be interested in how it turns out. If they resist, impose a consequence and insist that they try again.

For example, you've told the kids to decide between themselves which TV show to watch and when—you'll be back in five minutes for their answer. Five minutes go by and they're still arguing. Kiss the TV time goodbye. After an hour of silence, they will try again. This is sometimes referred to as "military justice." Either everyone learns to cooperate and solve problems rapidly, or everyone faces the same consequence. Tough and fair.

Now to be fair, it is a good idea to meet with each child separately after the squabble is over so that you can find out what happened and prevent one child from bullying the other. If you know beyond a doubt that one kid was the victim of the other, you can return to the offender and say, "This is the truth as I know it to be," and then follow through accordingly with any additional consequences.

These techniques are very effective tools to compel people to solve disputes. Suddenly, the kids are in a life raft and they must now head toward the
shore or sink. The kids will learn very quickly that it is not a good idea to
have a knife fight in a rubber raft. Children learn very quickly to row.

REWARDING POSITIVE BEHAVIOR

One last thing about sibling fighting. You will increase your odds of success
in eliminating sibling fighting by using rewards to deter it. Parents can use
the point system by awarding each sibling points for the day for choosing not
to get into hassles with each other to the point that the parents become
involved. I would especially recommend the use of the "unconditional" reward. When you take notice of your kids observing the rules about sibling
fighting—and they are being cooperative, helpful, and pleasant to one another—give them an unplanned and unexpected reward. Along with the other
skills described above, it will help greatly in siblings learning to be brothers
and sisters, and you'll have peace and quiet. Peace and quiet enough for the
kids to search the encyclopedia about Bolivian exports.

Chapter Twenty-Two

Stealing

Sample consequences rules: Never steal. Never take anything that does not belong to you. Always pay for every item. Always get permission to take someone else's things.

Very young children have no concept of stealing. They see it, they want it, they take it because it's "mine." They must be taught that taking things that do not belong to them is wrong. Children and teenagers take things that don't belong to them for one obvious reason: they want it (or think that they do) and stealing is the way to get it. Stealing can also be a means to an end: money for things they should not have, activities, or things to buy. Stealing is much like lying in that stealing is only of practical value to the child if he can get away with it consistently. Conversely, the natural, logical, and active consequences for stealing work much as they do for lying. In fact, lying and stealing often go hand-in-hand. If you see evidence of one, you may need to look for evidence of the other.

If you want stealing to cease, you need a zero-tolerance policy toward stealing in any form. This is simply one offense that you will not tolerate. You must reject any rationalizations for stealing: "everybody does it," "it's just a little item," "the stores can afford it," "they'll never miss it," "I 'found' it," "so and so 'gave' it to me," or "and I suppose you don't cheat on your taxes?"

LOGICAL CONSEQUENCES

If your child steals do not shame, discuss, or moralize about stealing—he or she knows it's wrong. If the child is caught stealing, the best logical consequence is to have him pay restitution. This could involve returning the item or money with an apology, paying the cost to the victims in the form of a refund, or, when these are not possible, working for the cost of the items and donating the money to charity. If the child is arrested and becomes involved with the juvenile justice authorities, their consequences should be implemented hand-in-hand with yours.

Other consequences for stealing can be loss of privileges for the day on which the stealing occurred, with only basic privileges for the following weekend. If your child is already on restriction or level system (chapter 5), then use the restitution approach in addition to the loss of freedom. If the stealing is significant in terms of value, use the six-day level system.

ACTIVE CONSEQUENCES

For the habitual thief, these consequences will typically have little practical effect for very long. Chances are good that you'll need to implement all five of the active consequences to deter stealing. Start with telling the young thief that only the adults in her life—parents, teachers, and the like—will be permitted to be the judges of what is stealing. They may label an act as stealing by witnessing it, having it reported to them, or noting that something is missing. Nor can the child "borrow" or "use" someone else's things. If she doesn't want to be accused of stealing, then her behavior needs to be above reproach.

Intercession

You may also want to consider enrolling your child in a therapy program for habitual stealers (check with your county's mental health agencies or on the Internet), or have her see a private therapist. Most children who steal are not calculating safecrackers, and most thieves aren't very good at it. Kids who steal frequently do so to meet an emotional need and on an impulse. Counseling programs can teach kids how to resist the impulse and meet the emotional need in other ways.

Networking

Networking with the adults in your child's life is critical. It is much harder to steal when someone is looking over your shoulder. Also, do not leave items that can be carried off easily—such as cash, cigarettes, alcohol, jewelry, and car keys—unattended in the house or with your personal things. You'll only fuel the stealing habit. Request that members of the network be mindful of these things when the child is with them.

Tracking

Consistently track what your child has possession of and whether he has a receipt for each item. If he cannot produce a receipt for an item, it goes back to where it came from, or, when that is not possible, it is donated to charity. In some cases you can advertise a possession—such as the new just-her-size leather boots that she "found" in a box in a field—until you locate the rightful owner.

Monitoring and Supervision

Monitor or supervise the child's opportunities to steal. For example, do not permit your child to shop in stores unless she is under eyeball supervision. Stealing not only goes along with unsupervised time and situations but also with *wandering*. Children who steal habitually wander about town, school, and the neighborhood. They also strive to get just as much time away from adult supervision as they can. Put the brakes on wandering by monitoring consistently. Know the basics: whom they are with, where they are, and what they are doing.

REWARDING POSITIVE BEHAVIOR AND OVERCORRECTION

We want to reward the positive opposite behavior of stealing—which is, of course, not stealing. Use overcorrection to "practice" not stealing in given situations. For example, going to the grocery store without taking things, paying for them, having the receipt and coming home with the correct change and the items that you sent them for. Do praise your child when they bring you receipts, and there are no reports or suspicion of stealing. You can also use the point system or contracts to provide formal rewards. Instead of Billy stealing money to buy a new skateboard, he can in time earn the money by not stealing, and have the freedom to spend all day Saturday at the skate park with his friends. It is easy for any kid to see which is the better choice.

As stealing behavior starts to decrease (and it will with consistent application of these skills) you will be able to restore or extend more freedom to your child as well. Your child can be successful at any number of things. Stealing is just not one of them. Stealing may occur no matter how many possessions he has, how much money he may have, how much he knows better, or how much he is loved. But it will stop if you follow through consistently to make it so.

Chapter Twenty-Three

Swearing

Sample consequence rules: Never swear. Never use foul, crude, dirty, vulgar, or obscene language. Never use foul or abusive language that is directed at someone else.
Natural consequence: Child experiences unpleasant interactions with people as a result of swearing.
Logical consequences: Parent walks away from the child when he/she swears or uses abusive language. Parent ignores the swearing. Response cost.
Active consequences: Confiscation, argument deflectors (see "Arguing"), networking, modeling, and intercession.

Most people swear out of either habit or anger. Children swear for these two reasons and to establish a position with their parents—that they can shock them, defy them, can't be controlled by them, or that they are really an adult who can swear if they want to.

Salty language has lost its saltiness. From the outhouse to the White House, swearing has become commonplace, and, for the most part, socially acceptable. People don't swoon any longer when they hear a child swearing. In many minds, it's okay.

Given this, and if swearing is commonplace in your home, it will be tough to enforce a consequence rule for the use of bad language. If you or others do it, why can't they? The answer may be because it is not desirable, morally acceptable, or permissible for children to engage in this behavior. Or you may decide that in the overall scheme of things, concern about your child using foul language is a low priority. If you do think it's important, is there anything you can do? But of course.

NATURAL CONSEQUENCES

The natural consequence is to permit the child to experience the disapproval and anger of people who are offended at his offensive language and to let him deal with these people on his own. This intervention is usually only effective with kids who swear infrequently, or spend a lot of time around saints.

The second most common advice from parent educators for dealing with swearing is twofold: walk away from the child when he swears or ignore the behavior (most parent educators don't recommend washing mouths out with soap, as this is viewed as a relic of nineteenth-century grandmothers). Walking away from a swearing child is a good idea—especially if he is swearing for your listening pleasure. However, this intervention only works if the kid *wants* you to be with him. If he doesn't, and he swears to get you to walk away, then he has developed a handy tool to control your whereabouts. Ignoring swearing usually only works for very young children. Older children are wise to you when you ignore them.

RESPONSE COST

Some years ago an American army intelligence officer was serving in Vietnam. He was upset because his troops were bringing him enemy prisoners who had been beaten. He told his men that for every prisoner found to have bruises, he would subtract one day from the soldiers' rest and relaxation time, and he would add one day for every prisoner who had no marks. The colonel started getting prisoners who were—as one soldier told me—"showered, shaved, and dressed in tuxedos." Psychologists call this behavior modification technique "response cost." For every "wrong" response you make, you lose; for every "right" response, you win. This is probably the single most effective technique to deter children from swearing, and to encourage its opposite.

These penalties can take a number of forms: losing money, time, privileges, or favors. Some parents have subtracted money from the child's allowance for swearing, and have donated the money to charity in the child's name. Some parents have used short groundings, work details, or taking away privileges as forfeiture for swearing or using abusive language, with apologies as needed.

I think the single best use of response cost is the losing of favors. Most parents gladly do many favors for their kids: drive them to the mall or to their friends' house, provide money for entertainment, do chores and run errands, and so forth. You can tell your child: "If you do not do what I want, I will not do what you want. If you choose not to follow the rule about swearing by swearing, I will subtract one favor I do for you from a list of favors."

This technique works especially well for children in the habit of swearing at you, the parent. It also is very effective if the child uses backtalk, or says something to you that is insulting or insolent. (Of course, it doesn't work in the *least* if you are modeling the behavior of swearing at the child or saying things to *them* that are insulting or insolent.)

When swearing occurs, do not count the number of words, count the incident; otherwise you could wind up in absurdity.

"Let's see, that was five *#^@! and four #^&%$."

"No, Dad, I said four {#&^ and five #^&%$."

"Oh, right, thanks dear."

INTERCESSION

Other techniques that might prove to be of value include some intercession skills. Just as you have taught them manners, teach your child that some people do not like or are offended by crude language. Your child may not think it is offensive, but others do. Further, some people will think you are ignorant and rude and not worthy of their time and attention because of swearing. This reaction could be especially costly if it is someone your child wants to impress—that cute girl in math class perhaps, or a prospective mentor or valued adult. Tell your child that no one outside of a small circle of dolts will think he is cool, sophisticated, or smart because he can swear. Any fool can do it—and frequently does. Your child says, "Okay, I can't swear; so what am I supposed to do when I'm mad?" One father I know taught his children to use alternative swearing: God *bless*; that's *bovine excrement!* this is all *mucked* up; and the like. As silly as this sounds it worked wonders for that family. Further, it serves to illustrate the stupidity of being unable to speak the language without swearing.

A more practical suggestion may be to take your child to a therapist or counselor experienced in habit and anger control so that he or she can learn the skills necessary to eliminate a ridiculous habit, and to refrain from getting angry without cause. Swearing is a learned behavior and a habit. What is learned can be unlearned, and a habit, any habit, can be reversed in about three weeks.

PRAISE AND REWARDS

Like any number of behaviors you want to pinpoint and target for change, you can take notice and praise your child for not swearing in instances when she has typically done so. You can also use the point system to reward her for holding her tongue by not swearing, backtalking, or saying something nasty to someone.

MODELING

When children are young, parents frequently attempt to control or curtail their own swearing around their children for fear that they'll "pick it up" and embarrass their parents. Why stop exercising restraint when your child becomes older? Model the behavior that you want to see repeated and don't swear around your kids. This will be hard for some of us—myself included—but it certainly can be done. By listening to their parents swear, kids learn that it's okay to swear—not that it's right or preferable to do, but that it's okay—Dad does it, so does Mom, it's not that big a deal. Further, if you have strong moral or religious convictions about swearing, then your child needs to hear that as well.

MORE CONSEQUENCES

If swearing is accompanied by arguing turn aside his rants by using argument deflectors and clouding. If the loss of favors used in response cost is ineffective, use confiscation or forfeiture to help him get a handle on swearing. Network with all the adults in your child's life to get reports about swearing when he is not with you. Won't that become absurd? Yes, it will. And when your child gets tired of swearing and being penalized for it, he will give it up.

The end result of these interventions is that when your child isn't overtaken by anger and frustration and habit, he can be a calm, cool cat who doesn't swear because he has no need for it. This will impress people far more than all the obscenities a kid could recite in a month of Sundays.

Chapter Twenty-Four

Television and Video Games

Sample consequence rules: Only watch programs that you have permission to watch. Complete all of your chores and homework before watching TV. Never watch _____.
Natural consequence: Child may be adversely influenced by the content of the program he/she is watching.
Logical consequence: Parent limits the number of hours of TV the child can watch. Parent restricts access to certain television programs.
Active consequences: Networking, monitoring, and supervision.

Television programs exist to sell products. We all know that. In order to sell us products television writers and producers must produce programs that hold our interest. That is why there is so much violence, sex, and lurid detail on television—it holds our interest. It holds our children's interest, too. The average child watches three hours of television every day. The TV shows children watch range widely from such positive fare as educational programs for preschoolers, to programs and movies that are carpet-bombed with crude language, mayhem, and sexual content. Exactly the same is true for video games, including ones that are only supposed to be played by adolescents and adults.

There are no research studies that positively prove kids are more likely to become violent, sexual, or salacious because of exposure to TV programs. And there are no research studies that positively prove that they are not, too. Certainly, both children and adults are influenced by what they see on TV; otherwise, advertising would be pointless. Exactly to what extent people are prone to imitate what they see on the screen, no one knows for sure. It is very difficult to show a direct cause-and-effect relationship in correlation studies, especially with kids. If you really don't care what your child wants to watch on TV, or if you're satisfied that your child consistently makes good choices about what to watch on TV, then don't make TV an issue. If you do want to limit your child's television choices, what can you do? Quite a lot, actually.

Intercession

Some parents make a habit of allowing their child to watch certain shows but consistently discuss the content of the shows with them. You may want to explain that yes, everyone on this soap opera has premarital, extramarital, between marital, and no marital sex, but this is fantasy, pure and simple. Most people do not behave this way.

Explain further that the values presented in what the characters do and how they treat each other reflect the writer's, producer's, and performer's values. If it is the case, point out that these are *your* family values about sexual and ethical behavior. The same goes for violent content. Squealing tires, blazing guns, flying fists, and exploding debris—along with sexual gymnastics—are plot devices that are cheap substitutes for the effort of presenting real human drama. Keep in mind that the producers, writers, performers, and advertisers don't give a flip about your child's moral development or the content of their character. In response to criticism, they say that is the parent's job; their job is to entertain and make money. They are right. It is the parents' job to teach our children well.

Monitoring

What can you do if you do not want your child watching vulgar comedians, heads being bashed in with metal chairs, mayhem and blood splattering, or cross-dressing skinheads who love Elvis on talk shows? You can go through the TV guide and mark the shows that your child is permitted to watch—which is the honor system. You can monitor and supervise what and when they watch by watching with him or her. You can program, or have your TV programmed to block offensive content, pay-per-view, adult channels, and the like, if you wish. All newer TVs have the "V" chip, which can be easily programmed to prevent your kids from watching certain shows during unsupervised hours. There are devices that only allow a TV to be operated during certain hours. Some parents have locked up the TV in the closet during unsupervised times, or disabled the TV during these times. A few parents have given the TV the boot.

If your child is fortunate enough to have a TV of their own in their bedroom, don't forget to use the "V" chip in their TV as well. However, you should encourage your child to watch TV with the family at least some of the time. If a kid spends all of their free time alone in their room with electronic gadgets, they are in danger of developing emotional attachments with the TV and other machines that can substitute for emotional attachments with the family.

NETWORKING

Well, what if your kid will just skip over to her friend's house or the neighbor's to watch the forbidden program there? Network with the adults in that home. Explain that your child does not have permission to watch certain programs or play certain video games and ask for their cooperation. Most adults will be glad to give it.

GOODBYE TV

Actively seek to get the kids habituated off TV. Limit the number of hours and programs the kids can watch each day. Provide stimulating conversation, books to read, plays to see, concerts and recitals to attend, exhibits to tour, activities to engage in, sports and games to play, places to go, and people to see instead.

If you need to, include rewards for non-TV time in the point system. A child who has never been can earn points for attending a play, or for reading a classic novel. They may like it so much that you can discontinue the point system quickly, as TV becomes a lost interest.

The TV pipeline can provide many wonderful programs to enlighten and entertain. It can also operate as an open sewer. We must use our discretion and good sense in helping children become discriminating viewers.

Chapter Twenty-Five

Truancy and Misbehavior in School

Sample consequence rules: Attend every class that you are enrolled in every day school is in session. Stay in class for the entire class session. Follow all of the classroom rules and meet all behavior expectations.
Natural consequence: Child fails the subject or grade because of missing too many classes. Child fails the subject or grade because of habitual disruptive behavior in class.
Logical consequence: Child studies at home during free time for the number of hours truant. Child studies at home for one hour for every school reported instance of disruptive behavior in school.
Active consequences: Intercession, networking, supervision, shadowing, and Forfeiture Day.

Playing hooky is a time-honored tradition in American education. Almost all kids skip a class or a day once in a while. This doesn't make the practice right, just commonplace. The practice is rare in elementary school, but becomes more frequent when kids enter middle school. Being disruptive in school is as old as school itself. If the child is habitually truant, you'll need to use a consequence rule with a set consequence. The same is true if your child is consistently disruptive in school.

LOGICAL AND ACTIVE CONSEQUENCES

The natural consequence is of no value to the truant or disruptive child. All it does is let him fail. The logical consequence of studying at home for the number of hours missed, or attending makeup classes, are very valuable because they teach the importance of time and responsibility. Some schools have in-school detention, after-school class, or Saturday school for truants, late attendees, and disruptive students. Some schools use temporary time-out isolation for children who are disruptive in class. If so, a boring Saturday school or in-school or after-school detention can deter many truants and misbehaving students.

ACTIVE CONSEQUENCES

Shadowing involves going to school with your child: escorting the habitual truant to each class, sitting with a misbehaving student in class, and following him around school by going to the lunchroom and riding the bus with him or her if need be. Shadowing is an overcorrection technique—attending and performing in class until they have it right. The active consequence of shadowing for truancy is very effective—no child wants their mom or dad walking him or her from class to class or sitting with him in class directing their behavior—but should be used as the *last* consequence. It gives you a place to go if the logical consequence is disregarded. The shadowing technique also works well to deter the child who plays the brat, the buffoon, or the bully while at school. Rarely will you need to do this more than *once*.

What if you can't go to school or your child actively rebels? Consider hiring a *friendly gorilla* to accompany your child to school, sit with your child in class, and in the lunchroom, and accompany him to the bathroom (same sex gorilla, of course). Or maybe the gorilla rides the school bus home with your child and sits with him while he does his homework at the kitchen table. You can also network with other parents to hire an "on call" gorilla— such as a parent volunteer, or you can enlist the help of a relative or family friend for this task.

If you cannot find anyone to help you, consider hiring an escort service for the day (not that kind of escort service). There are professional youth escort services whose job it is to transport unwilling kids to psychiatric hospitals and treatment centers. For a fee they may be willing to consider escorting your child to all of his classes or to be with him while he is in class.

Also, see if you can enlist the support of a vice principal, the police liaison officer at your child's school, or the school's security team to help you track and monitor your child's activities and whereabouts during the school day. Ask if one of them could escort your child to class.

What if your child shoots out the back door of the school or refuses to go to school the next day after period cuts? Tell her that you'll be back until the day of shadowing is completed. What if your child says that they'll be glad to have you come to class the next day? She will not be so glad when she sees and hears the reaction of her classmates.

Forfeiture Day

As an alternative to shadowing, you can use what I call Forfeiture Day. The next available free day the child has from school is forfeited. The child spends the equivalent number of hours or days that he was truant or disruptive completing work projects on his day off (without compensation). You can also arrange that he do a half-day of schoolwork (Saturday school at home) and a half-day of labor. Activities such as pulling weeds, cleaning the oven, and scrubbing the floors and toilets should do nicely.

Another alternative is to take your child to work with you (or send him to work with a trustworthy adult) and have him sit for the day. There is no reading (other than schoolwork), TV, music, games, phone calls, text messaging, conversation, or other forms of engagement—he just sits where you keep an eye on him and reads his social studies text and does algebra problems.

NETWORKING

Establish a personal network with someone in the school administration that you can talk to on an as-needed basis. You want to be made aware of even one cut class or disruptive behavior incident every time it occurs. Ask for a same-day telephone call with information that you need: which period or periods were skipped, what was the disruptive behavior, and/or if the child was seen in other locations. If a teacher sent the child out of the room, find out why. What if you think the child will intercept the call or your voice mail or dispose of any mailed written messages? What if you can't be called at work? Ask a friend or relative to take the calls for you or to receive written notices from the school. You can also use a post office box, cell phone, fax, text, or email messages to electronic devices.

REWARDS

It is easy to pinpoint the behavior that you want to see changed. It is in the sample consequence rules. Tell your child that you will use any of these techniques to stop truancy and misbehavior in class. Also, they can avoid the negative consequences *and* earn positive rewards for the positive behavior of regular school attendance and positive behavior in class with contracting or the point system.

INTERCESSION

What if your child refuses to attend school because of an emotional problem, an issue with a teacher, that they are being harassed, bullied, or threatened, or the inability to do the work? What if they are involved in antisocial activity? Find out precisely what the problem is and then provide the necessary intervention (see "School Assignments and Homework").

What if he says, "School is boring; all the teachers are a bunch of jerks; besides, you don't pass if you attend class and do the work, 'cause it depends on if they like you or not." Such claims are an invitation to a dance—the dance of arguing. When your child starts singing this tune—don't dance. Instead, deflect the argument (see "Arguing") and then help get her ready for school.

Chapter Twenty-Six

Whereabouts and Curfews

Sample consequence rules: Observe all curfew laws. Be home for the night by specified times. Always ask permission before leaving one location and going to another.
Natural consequence: At risk for arrest, assault, or injury.
Logical consequence: Loss of out-of-the-house freedom for a specified period of time.
Active consequences: Networking, monitoring, and tracking.

As children get older and feel a need for independence, they want to spend increasingly longer periods of time out of the house and away from their parents. This is as it should be. Most kids can handle the freedom and can make appropriate decisions for themselves. Such older children are rightly permitted to do what they choose and to come home when they like   within reason.

If you don't set a curfew for them, the city or county where you live has likely already done so. The reason is simply because it is not safe or desirable for kids to be out late without a legitimate reason, or unless they are under responsible adult supervision. In some communities, there are daytime curfew laws during the school day, as well as those at night. Like it or not, the government does regulate parenting to some extent. Since the government may step in, it is important that we know what the laws are in our community regarding age-limit curfew, and make certain that our children follow those laws.

Supervision and Networking

If your kids are going to be out at night, possibly up to the time of the curfew, then they should be in "confined" areas: at a responsible adult's job site, in an approved home, at a movie theater or skating rink, at a Friday night football game, and so on, where there is at least some semblance of adult supervision. Kids are especially at risk while cruising on the streets or standing on street corners talking to their friends late at night. This is not to say the kids should never be allowed to congregate with their friends at night—it is to say that they are at greater risk for harm when unsupervised.

You may live in a community where drive-by shootings, drunken fights, robberies, rapes, and drug deals are nonexistent, or you may live in a community where they are common. These activities almost always happen under the cover of darkness and fear, and innocent children can find themselves caught in the crossfire. It only has to happen once for your child to be maimed or killed.

Most juvenile crime (and sexual activity) takes place between the hours of 3:00 and 6:00 in the afternoon. Obviously, this is when most kids are out of school and away from adult supervision. If you have reason to believe that your child needs supervision to avoid trouble, consider enrolling him or her in after-school activities, or signing them up for late afternoon activities sponsored by programs such as those at community centers, the Boys and Girls Club, or YMCA. Some churches and religious centers also offer supervised activities for your child.

If your child refuses to go, or you cannot find a suitable site, alert the network to keep an eye on things. Perhaps your neighbor will be willing to report comings and goings at your house. Or you can make arrangements with a trusted parent of one of your child's friends to help you. Some parents in networks agree to take turns "patrolling" homes of kids in the network, driving by or ringing the doorbell to see what is going on. You can also hire a house sitter for the hours you are gone and can't supervise. In recent times there are computer-based programs available that allow you to have cameras installed at your house to see who has come in and gone out, who is there, and what they are doing in common areas of the house.

Should you ever compromise on curfew times? Compromise should be the exception, not the rule. Kids know, as in most things, that if you compromise once you can be persuaded to do so again. There is also nothing wrong with using common sense regarding curfew. Younger kids should have an earlier curfew than older ones, and irresponsible kids need a tighter curfew than responsible ones.

Preventative Supervision

What if your kid continuously disregards curfew or sneaks out of the house at night? If you have an idea where your child might be, don't wait for him or her to come home—go and get them. Alternatively, if you can make phone contact requesting a trustworthy adult—such as the friend's parents—help ensure that they safely leave for home immediately, that is fine too.

If your child is in the habit of not telling others where he is going, require a name, address, and phone number that is *verified* before he can go out again. You might also consider putting your child on the level system (chapter 5) until he or she shows signs of improvement. If your child is one who habitually "forgets" what time it is, have him carry a pager or cell phone (at her allowance expense for the device or minutes purchased) so that you can electronically alert her when it is time to come home. Some parents also use Global Positioning Systems (GPS) to track their child's whereabouts. These devices can locate a person's whereabouts within feet of where they are standing.

Should the child who habitually sneaks out of the bedroom window at night have a window that opens? You don't need iron bars and attack dogs, but you need to secure the bedroom window from the inside. In certain cases, you can go so far as to have your child sleep in your bedroom at night in a sleeping bag, or you can install door knob alarms or home security systems to keep her in at night, but don't forget to have smoke alarms and exit plans for fire safety. Until when? Until the child's nighttime wanderlust ceases.

Monitoring

Finally, for the generally trustworthy older child who needs to be home by a certain time, don't stay up late waiting for him. Make notifying you solely the child's responsibility. Here is how: tell him that you have an alarm clock set for his curfew time set just inside your bedroom door. It's his job to turn off the alarm before the curfew time arrives. If you are awakened, you will be grumpy when he gets home and may restrict him from going out again. Having to make a mad dash to turn off the alarm before it wakes you up may help the child learn to be punctual. If you think a sibling may be enlisted to turn off the alarm for the wayward child, a kiss on the cheek will do. If that would disturb your sleep, have your child leave his wallet and house keys by your bed.

For the generally untrustworthy child who needs to be home by a certain time, here is what you do: require him or her to take a photograph of him or herself using a digital or cell phone camera. The camera will record the date and time the picture was taken. Specify that the picture inside the house include some prominent feature in the background. If you think a wily kid will sneak back out of the house, install a security system and then set the system to be activated a few minutes past the scheduled curfew time.

It can be fun and useful for older kids to be out and away from their parents some of the time—kids need the practice of making good choices while on their own. We as parents need the practice of letting them go; what we want is for them to practice safety as we let them go.

Epilogue

You now have two strong hands to work with to accomplish the behavior change you want to see in your child. On the right hand, you have discipline skills, contracting, and the point system. The discipline skills stop and prevent negative, unwanted behavior, and the reward system encourages and strengthens positive, wanted behaviors. When used in tandem, the discipline skills and the reward system will quickly and effectively change behavior. However, the changes will not *last* without the skills of the left hand. On the left hand, you have communication and problem-solving skills. When used in an atmosphere of love and praise, you will greatly strengthen the parent-child relationship.

Do not be tempted to put your emphasis on only one set of skills. Discipline without encouragement will not work; love without discipline will not work; and relationships without work will not work. To do that would be like trying to sit at a table where one of the four legs is too long or too short. The imbalance invites disaster. *When the skills of the right hand and the left hand are in balance, they work wonders.*

Parenting skills are like any other skill. You must practice them until they become a natural part of your being. If you do not see the behavior change you want, stay with it. Your child did not acquire negative behavior overnight and it will not change overnight. Change frequently arrives in small, incremental steps that can be celebrated and built upon.

Kids are as changeable as the wind direction. Change will come. The great thing about the strategies presented in this book is that you will see change before your eyes.

Let's say you have started a discipline plan to stop your child's bullying. You have established a consequence rule and provided intercession. You have begun tracking, monitoring, and networking with the adults in his life.

You have communicated with him about your concerns and problem-solved strategies for him to say *no* to his friends and others who may encourage this behavior. You have set up a point system with rewards and praise for evidence of not bullying. You have shown him how much he is loved. The result is a decrease in bullying and abandonment of it in a short time.

Kids respond to their parents' demands when they see that their parents are serious about behavior change and will follow through consistently to make it happen. They respond to their parents' demands because they have a loving relationship that they value and do not wish to see disrupted.

I have a daughter whom I love with all my might. I know that you feel the same way about your child or children. Loving them with all our might means doing everything in our power to teach, guide, protect, nurture, direct, correct, and empower them to be and to have every good thing. Do practice the strategies and skills in this book. Your child will have every good thing come to them.

—Michael Hammond

Suggested Readings

Bodenhamer, Gregory. *Back in Control: How to Get Your Children to Behave*. New York: Fireside, 1983. This older book details a number of useful ideas about parenting children with difficult behavior.

Chamberlain, Patricia. *Family Connections*. Eugene, OR: Northwest Media, 1998. This book contains several excellent examples of point system economies and level systems.

Dreikurs, Rudolf, and Vicki Soltz. *Children: The Challenge*. New York: Duell, Sloane, and Pearce, 1963. This classic book in the parenting literature explains the origin of the concepts of natural and logical consequences.

Kazdin, Alan. *Parent ManagementTraining* New York: Oxford University Press, 2005. Dr. Kazdin explains common behavioral parenting techniques, some of which are presented for practical use in this book.

McKay, Matthew, Martha Davis, and Patrick Fanning. *Messages: The Communications Skills Book*. Oakland, CA: New Harbinger, 1995. A classic book on improving interpersonal communication techniques.

Index